OVERTAKE AND RECOVER ALL

Power Must Change Hands Vol. 2

Godson T. Nembo

IEM PRESS

PURSUE, OVERTAKE AND RECOVER ALL

Power Must Change Hands Vol. 2

Copyright © September 2012
Godson T. Nembo

ISBN-13: 978-1-947662-23-0

For more information:
www.christianrestorationnetwork.org
www.facebook.com/godsontnembo
Email: info@christianrestorationnetwork.org

Or write to:
Tangumonkem Godson Nembo
P.O. Box 31339 Biyem Assi Yaounde – Cameroon
Tel.: (237) 674.495.895 or 699.902.618

IEM PRESS is honored to present this title with the
author. The views expressed or implied in this work
are those of the author. IEM Press provides our
imprint seal representing design excellence,
creative content and high-quality production.

To learn more about IEM Press visit
www.iempublishing.com

All scripture quotations are from the New King James Version (NKJV) of the Bible, except otherwise stated.

DEDICATION

This book is dedicated to my wife; Anna Nama Tangumonkem. You have been a very faithful prayer partner for all these years.

CONTENTS

DEDICATION.. iv

INTRODUCTION ix

Part 1: PREPARING TO PRAY 13

   Chapter 1: GENERAL INSTRUCTIONS 15

   Chapter 2: THE POWER OF FASTING 21

   Chapter 3: HOW TO DELIVER YOURSELF 37

   Chapter 4: HOW TO FIND A QUALIFIED
             DELIVERANCE MINISTER 47

   Chapter 5 51

   DELIVERANCE QUESTIONNAIRE 51

Part 2: PRAYER MARATHON 67

   Chapter 6: PROPHETIC DECLARATIONS OVER
             YOUR LIFE....................................... 69

      DAY 1: CONSECRATION................................. 72

DAYS 2-3: PURSUE, OVERTAKE AND
RECOVER ALL 79

DAYS 4-5: ANOINTING FOR TOTAL
RECOVERY 87

DAYS 6-7: THE POWER OF SACRIFICE 97

DAYS 8-9: THE KEY OF SACRIFICE 104

DAYS 10-11: IDENTIFYING
STRONGHOLDS 114

DAYS 12-13: PULLING DOWN
STRONGHOLDS 122

DAY 14: BREAKING THE YOKE OF FEAR 1 130

DAY 15: BREAKING THE YOKE OF FEAR 2 140

DAY 16: IDENTIFYING NEGATIVE INHERITED
PATTERNS 147

DAY 17: BREAKING NEGATIVE INHERITED
PATTERNS 158

DAYS 18-19: BREAKING CURSES 1 169

DAY 20: BREAKING CURSES 2 185

DAY 21: FREEDOM FROM SOUL TIES 197

DAY 22: DESTROYING EVIL SPIRITUAL
MARRIAGES 216

DAYS 23-24: SPIRITUAL REVIVAL IN THE
CHURCH AND THE NATION.. 229

DAYS 25-26: WAR AGAINST IDOLS 235

DAYS 27: BE HEALED! 247

DAY 28: BREAKING THE YOKE OF POVERTY
    AND STAGNATION..........................253

DAY 29: ANOINTING FOR EXPLOITS..........262

DAY 30: THANKSGIVING AND
    TESTIMONIES...................................276

BIBLE READING PLANS **278**

SOURCES CONSULTED: **280**

**OTHER CHRISTIAN RESTORATION NETWORK
PUBLICATIONS:** **282**

INTRODUCTION

This book, *"Power Must Change Hands Vol.2: Pursue, Overtake and Recover All"* is a prayer guide written for the Annual 30 Days Fast 2012. I believe that God has put it in your hands because He wants to do a unique work in your life. The annual fast has always been a time of multiple divine encounters that lead to multi-dimensional breakthroughs. As you read and pray with this book, the anointing of "Prayer Storm" will sweep through your life.

Anything you have lost on this planet can be recovered when the hand of God is released on your behalf. Usually people only go out on risky recovery missions when they have lost something, they consider to be very value. This book exposes different dimensions of blessings that have been stolen by the devil from individuals, families, churches, tribes and even nations. It shows you the way to total recovery. A profound knowledge of the blessings God has made available for you and how to access them will spare you from satanic manipulations.

When the time came for Moses to leave Egypt with the children of Israel in order to possess the Promised Land – a land flowing with milk and honey, Pharaoh tried to trap Moses into a terrible deal that would have forfeited their deliverance. First he told Moses and the people to worship God in the land and not to go far (Ex.8:25, 28). Second, he told them to go and worship alone leaving behind their wives and children (Ex.10:11). Third, he told them to go and worship leaving behind their flocks and herds (Ex.10:24). Moses vehemently refused to compromise. He told Pharaoh, *"Our livestock also shall go with us; not a hoof shall be left behind. For we must take some of them to serve the LORD our God, and even we do not know with what we must serve the LORD until we arrive there."* *(Ex.10:26)*. Moses understood that it was time to break out of slavery forever, so he refused to compromise with his enemy. The time has come for you to tell every Pharaoh in your life that all that is yours that has been in bondage must be released into your hands by force in the mighty name of Jesus.

"Power Must Change Hands" will usher you into a prophetic season of divine restoration. There is going to be a release of God's anointing in your life and family as a volcano. You will begin to see what you have never seen before. The greatest mistake the devil and his cohort have ever made is to have allowed you to pick up this book. I encourage you not to allow them use any scheme to cause you drop it. Read it thoroughly and pray all the prayers as a mad man or a mad woman. You will start recording unquestionable miracles as you begin reading and praying.

Each section of the book has prayer points to guide you pray. You should write out your own pray points as the Lord speaks to you through the teachings. Do not limit your prayers to the prayer points I have provided; also pray the ones you have noted.

Fasting draws our spirit man away from the pleasures of the flesh and connects us to the Holy Spirit for deeper spiritual experiences. As you fast, believe God to bring you into your jubilee. After these 30 days, your testimonies will be too many to be counted.

God bless you as you go through this great experience.

Rev. Tangumonkem Godson Nembo,
Bamenda –Cameroon 3rd September 2012

Part 1:

PREPARING TO PRAY

Chapter 1

GENERAL INSTRUCTIONS

These practical steps will help you to achieve greater results as you fast and pray for revival, restoration, healing and breakthrough for yourself, family, church and nation.

1. The first thing you need to do before you fast is set a definite time period for your fast. Will your fast be 1 meal, 3 days, 7 days, 21 days, 40 days? Do this to avoid being discouraged by the devil. It is also true that sometimes some people want to fast until they see divine intervention.

2. The second important thing you need to do is decide which type of fast you will undertake. Will it be a normal fast, a Daniel fast, or perhaps a television and entertainment fast, etc.? Some people decide to combine all.

3. If you are going on a long fast, please don't begin your fast immediately but rather gradually cut your food intake back and then begin your fast.

4. Cease drinking caffeine products a few days before you start a long fast so you can get over the withdrawal headaches before you start.

5. Drink warm water instead of cold and do not drink too much water at one time. Do not drink milk, coffee, or other beverages during the fast for this will be considered dieting and not fasting. (Follow these procedures on all types of fasts except the absolute fast.)

6. Add some drops of lemon in the water to improve the taste. The water helps to detoxify your body systems.

7. Do not take excessively hot baths during a prolonged fast; for this may cause dizziness. However, take a bath regularly during your fast because fasting causes many impurities to be secreted through the pores of your skin thus causing an odor.

8. Do not engage in excessive work or exercise during the fast.

9. If it is a dry fast, do not exceed 3 days without water. You can create problems to your body when you go for long without water.

10. Spend much time praying, reading and meditating on the word of God without which your fast could become a hunger strike.

11. Use the prayer points in this book as a guide and also add yours as the Holy Spirit leads you.

12. Pray the word of God. Do this by using Bible verses to re-enforce your prayer.

13. Be attentive to what the Holy Spirit is saying and make sure note in your diary.

14. Settle any disputes before you start fasting. Disputes, bitterness and un-forgiveness will block your prayers from reaching God. During and after the fast avoid quarrels and arguments.

15. Don't go around announcing to everyone that you are fasting (Matt.6: 16-17).

16. Wash yourself and be clean. Brush your teeth regularly and also use perfume if possible (there is bad odor released from the body during fasting).

17. If possible, pray with a prayer partner. If you have none pray alone.

18. Do not focus on the body weaknesses (the body is just reacting to the absence of food). Keep telling yourself, "It is well, I am an eagle".

19. Pray with expectation. God will not let you to seek Him in vain.

20. Make sacrifices (gifts and helps) during and after your fast.

21. Regarding sex during a fast, the Bible says:

"Do not deprive one another except with consent for a time, that you may give yourselves to fasting and prayer; and come together again so that Satan does not tempt you because of your lack of self-control." (1Cor.7:5).

It is not a sin to have sex during a fast when the two are in agreement. It is wrong to deprive your partner without his/her consent. It is best to stay away from sex in order to concentrate on the fast. Let the Holy Spirit guide you.

22. **Some Symptoms you May Experience During Fasting:**
The three phases of a prolonged fast are: Craving food; Feeling weak and faint for 2-3 days or even longer; and Growing stronger and no longer having concern about food.

Some symptoms you may experience are headache, nausea, low fever, sleeplessness, and stomach pains. If you have any of these symptoms do not take medication for them. If you have any of these symptoms do not take medication for them.

23. **Breaking the fast:**
Breaking the fast is the most difficult period after the fast; it requires discipline and self-control. If you fast for many days, then you should allow your body an adequate period of time to recover so you will be able to resume your regular diet.

Start with some vegetable and fruit juices a little at a time and maybe a cup of watered-down soup. The following day, start to drink juices and increase the thickness of the soup. Continue to do this until you gradually begin to build yourself back up.

Our Lord Jesus Christ fasted for 40 days while He lived in a human body. You too can practice fasting even if not for 40 days as Jesus did.

Chapter 2

THE POWER OF FASTING

The spiritual power that is released through fasting and prayer can only be likened to atomic power.

Those who know how to tap this power are doing exploits. Satanists know this so they fast to open their lives to satanic power. We got information that Satanists gathered in South Africa to fast for the destruction of the families of believers. It is recorded that after the fast, many marriages of believers and even those of some top ministers of the gospel collapsed woefully. A few months ago, I prayed with a girl from Bafoussam who told me that some time ago, she fasted for 40 days just to acquire powers to destroy some families. After her fast, she killed some people, even her family members. I read the testimony of a man who fasted for one year in order to be able to see Lucifer.

Other religious adherents like Buddhists, Hindus and Moslems also fast regularly. Medical practitioners recommend fasting for the cleansing of the body. A woman told me some years ago that her doctor placed her on a three day fast after which she regained her health without drugs.

The Lord gave me this mandate to fast for 30 days every year (to pray for a move of God in the church and for the nation of Cameroon) in the year 2001. By the grace of God, I have been doing it faithfully till today. I cannot explain in a book what God has done in my life and ministry during all these years. It was during the tenth edition that the Lord told me to involve other people in the program. Many who participated have shared with us many testimonies of healings, deliverances and breakthroughs. You too will have your own testimony as you fast in Jesus' name.

Remember that even animals, insects and birds practice fasting. When the caterpillar prepares to move to the next stage (butterfly), it goes into a season of fasting. The eagle also fasts in order to improve on its ability to fly faster and higher. Snakes fast when they want to shed their skin in order to grow fatter; you too can fast.

WHAT IS FASTING?

Fasting is going without food or water in order to seek God. When you stay without food and do not pray that can be called a hunger strike and not fasting. You must set aside ample time during your fast to wait on the Lord. Fasting is a form of spiritual discipline that informs God that you are serious about repentance. Fasting is a significant part of your Christian walk just as praying and reading the Bible is significant. Fasting is for everyone who desires to draw closer to God. One of the most powerful weapons of spiritual warfare that God has given to His children is fasting. It is a way of crucifying the flesh or denying your flesh the basic sustenance of food. Although fasting will weaken you physically, it will highly enlighten you spiritually.

"But those who wait on the LORD shall renew their strength; They shall mount up with wings like eagles, They shall run and not be weary, They shall walk and not faint. (Isa.40:31).

When you fast, you do not have to give up just food; it can be anything of importance to you that is a sacrifice to give up.

Although fasting is not commanded in the Bible, it is expected of all believers in their Christian walk, for Matthew 6:17-18 says *"when you fast."* Jesus did not say, *"if you fast"* but rather *"when you fast'*; therefore Jesus reveals through scripture that fasting is expected of us; however, it is not commanded (for example, you are not committing sin by not fasting). But it becomes sin when you disobey the Holy Spirit by refusing to pray when He instructs you to do so.

TYPES OF FASTS

Normal Fast: This involves abstaining from all solid and liquid food except for water.

Absolute Fast: This involves abstaining from both food and drink. You should never stay on this fast more than three days, unless under the direction of the Holy Spirit.

Partial Fast: This involves abstaining from just certain foods. You can live on just certain foods during the duration of this fast such as bread and water, or you may choose to fast a certain meal each day.

Daniel Fast: This consists of fruits, vegetables, and water.

Juice Fast: This consists of fruit and vegetable juices only.

Others: Staying away from anything that that occupies your time to seek the face of God is also called a fast. You can fast from Television for a time in order to seek.

WHY SHOULD YOU FAST?

The prophet Isaiah writes:

"Is not this the fast that I have chosen? To loose the bands of wickedness, to undo the heavy burdens, and to let the oppressed go free, and that ye break every yoke? Is it not to deal thy bread to the hungry, and that thou bring the poor that are cast out to thy house? When thou seest the naked, that thou cover him; and that thou hide not thyself from thine own flesh?" Isaiah 58:6-7

Thus, there are 7 reasons for fasting according to Isaiah 58:6-7, and they are as follows:

1. To bring Justice.
2. To undo heavy burdens and break the yoke of bondage.
3. To free the oppressed and loose the bands of wickedness.
4. To share food.
5. To provide shelter for the poor.
6. To clothe the naked.
7. To provide for one's family.

However, there are several other reasons for fasting:

To Mourn and Repent:

You can set aside time to fast and pray to repent and amend your ways before God. You can also fast to pray to repent for the sins of your family, city, tribe and nation.

"In those days I Daniel was mourning three full weeks. I ate no pleasant bread, neither came flesh nor wine in my mouth, neither did I anoint myself at all, till three whole weeks were fulfilled." (Dan.10:2-3).

(Also see Esther 4:3; Isaiah 58:5; Joel 2:12-13; Zechariah 7:5)

To Receive God's Instructions:

In order to understand the perfect will of God concerning important decisions of your life it is necessary to wait before God in fasting. Fasting increases your spiritual sensitivity and enhances your abilities to catch signals in the spirit realm. It was during a period of fasting that Moses received the Ten Commandments.

"And he was there with the Lord forty days and forty nights; he did not eat bread, nor drink water. And he wrote upon the tables the words of the covenant, the ten commandments." Exodus 34:28 (Also see Acts 9:9-12; Acts 13:2)

To Die to the Flesh:

The Israelites fasted in those days to afflict their souls. This had to do with staying away from the pleasures of the flesh. Fasting helps to bring the desires of your flesh under control.

"Why have we fasted,' they say, 'and You have not seen? Why have we afflicted our souls, and You take no notice?' "In fact, in the day of your fast you

27

find pleasure, And exploit all your laborers."
(Isaiah 58:3).

Apostle Paul said,
**"But I discipline my body and bring it into
subjection, lest, when I have preached to others, I
myself should become disqualified." (1Cor.9:27).**

Bible scholars hold that the discipline Paul is talking
about here includes fasting.

For Humility and Deliverance from Bondage:

Fasting is a means to humble yourself before God
and to seek His face for divine intervention.

**"But as for me, when they were sick, my clothing
was sackcloth: I humbled soul with fasting; and
my prayer returned into mine own bosom."
(Psalm 35:13).**
(Also see I Samuel 7:3-14; Ezra 8:21-23).

For Health and Healing:

Fasting is therapeutic in that it helps in detoxifying
the human body. Just staying away from food and
drinking only water without praying has been
proven to be means to heal people from certain

diseases. The Bible makes it clear in Isaiah that fasting is means to facilitate your divine healing.

"Then your light shall break forth like the morning, Your healing shall spring forth speedily, And your righteousness shall go before you; The glory of the LORD shall be your rear guard." (Isa.58:8).
(Also see Psalm 35:13)

For Spiritual Power to Cast Out Demons:

Jesus Christ taught that fasting releasing power in the life of a believer to cast out demons.

"And Jesus rebuked the devil; and he departed out of him; and the child was cured from that very hour." Then came the disciples to Jesus apart, and said, Why could not we cast him out? And Jesus said unto them, 'Because of your unbelief: for verily I say unto you, if ye have faith as a grain of mustard seed, ye shall say unto this mountain, remove hence to yonder place; and it shall remove; and nothing shall be impossible unto you. Howbeit this kind goeth not out but by prayer and fasting.'" (Mat.17:18-21) KJV.

Sometimes when you have struggled with some cases of demonic possession and diseases and you cannot get a breakthrough, ask the Holy Spirit to guide you on how to confront the situation with fasting.

To seek God for Personal or Corporate Revival:

Fasting is one of the spiritual disciplines that will help rekindle the fire of the Holy Spirit in your life when you go into spiritual slumber. When an eagle becomes heavy and cannot fly higher and faster, it goes into a period of fasting after which it sheds away some of it feathers. After the fast, it is said that the eagle's strength increases greatly. It eye sight also improves as well as its flight speed.

Individual Christians and the Church as a whole need spiritual revival in our times. God has to release a mighty wave of holiness, power and renewal that will prepare the church as a bride for Jesus Christ. This wave of glory will also sweep thousands into the Kingdom of God. For this to happen we must fast and pray for ourselves, our families, our cities and our nation.

"Now, therefore," says the LORD, "Turn to Me with all your heart, With fasting, with weeping, and

with mourning. So rend your heart, and not your garments; Return to the LORD your God, For He is gracious and merciful, Slow to anger, and of great kindness; And He relents from doing harm. Who knows if He will turn and relent, And leave a blessing behind Him-A grain offering and a drink offering For the LORD your God? Blow the trumpet in Zion, Consecrate a fast, Call a sacred assembly; . . . Then the LORD will be zealous for His land, And pity His people." (Joel 2:12-18).

FASTING: THE NEGLECTED WEAPON:

While we cannot manipulate God to fulfill our desires, fasting always (when done the biblical way) moves God to fulfill his intended will over issues concerning us. Unfortunately, nowadays few Christians take fasting seriously. If we all would fast, there would be great revivals world over, breaking of bondages (yokes) in our lives and other people's lives. We also would be able to hear from God more clearly and the power of God will become very real among us.

I challenge you to use the weapon of fasting that has been the secret of all successful people of God. All men and women who impacted their generations with the power of God were men and women who fasted often. Kenneth Hagin senior who was mightily used of God and who fasted often wrote this in his book titled, *"A Common Sense Guide to Fasting:"*

"When I first went out in the field ministry, I set aside two days a week—Tuesday and Thursday—for my fast days. I wasn't led of the Lord to do it; I just fasted two days a week. I fasted 24 hours, because that was the way Israel did it. . . . I made the greatest spiritual strides yet in my ministry during that time of fasting two days a week. . . . After several years of fasting two days a week, the Lord said to me, "I would be more pleased if you would live a fasted life. I said, "What do you mean *a fasted life?"* He said, "Never eat all you want. Keep your appetite under. That's all a fast is going to do anyway, keep the body under." . . . Do you know that is harder than fasting? I changed. I never had any more *days* of fasting. I never set any times of fasting unless the Spirit of God spoke to me. And I made greater spiritual strides living *the fasted life.* Much of the time I ate only one meal a day while I was in meetings. (I still do that much of the time.) I noticed that healings came more easily when I did this. When it came to laying hands on people to receive the Holy Spirit, I wouldn't eat at all. If we'd run into a hard spot and things weren't happening like I thought they should,

I'd fast by drinking a little juice. If I needed more strength physically, I'd start eating, but I never ate all I wanted. I started having more results because I more or less constantly lived the fasted life."

HOW LONG SHOULD YOU FAST?

The Bible reveals to us how some saints of old fasted and the durations of their fasts. You can be inspired by their examples.

1. Jesus fasted 40 days without food to prepare for His public ministry (Mat.4:2). Many Bible scholars hold that He drank water since the Bible is silent about it.
2. Moses fasted twice for 40 days without food and water during which he received the 10 commandments
   (Deut.9:9, 18-19, Exo.34:27-28).
3. Elijah fasted for 40 days without food and water to meet with God (1Kgs.19).
4. Daniel fasted for 21 days eating light food and drinking water to seek for God's will concerning his people (Dan.9).
5. Paul, prisoners, and Roman troops fasted for 14 days without food for deliverance from deadly storms in the sea (Acts 27:33).
6. David fasted for 7 days without food to pray for his son who was sick (2Sam.12:16-20).

7. Esther fasted for 3 days without water and food to pray for the deliverance of Israel from Haman (Es.4).
8. Saul Fasted for 3 days after his conversion (9:9-12).
9. Nehemiah fasted to intercede for Israel. The Bible is silent about the number of days and the nature of the fast (Neh.1:4).
10. The Christians of Antioch fasted and prayed to minister to God. The Bible is silent about the duration and the nature of the fast (Acts 13:1-3).
11. John the Baptist's disciples fasted and prayed often. (Mark 2:18).

When it actually comes to determining how long you should fast, the Holy Spirit should be the one to guide you. If you are not careful, you can turn fasting into a religious activity. It will seem that God only moves when you have fasted. Kenneth Hagin Senior comments on this in his book *"The Common Sense Guide to Fasting"*:

"Some people try to make a religion out of fasting. They push themselves to an extreme, thinking *works* will get the job done. But I don't believe in *religion;* I believe in *Christ* and life in Christ. Don't get involved in works. Let the Lord lead you. Take some time to fast and wait on God *as the Spirit of God leads you.* Feel free to obey Him. I went to one place to hold revival, and we had the greatest revival in the history of that church. Sunday School doubled and church membership tripled. The pastor said night after night, "Boys, I just marvel at God moving in such a way. And we haven't even fasted."

Learn to listen to the voice of the Holy Spirit. Sometimes He will ask you to fast even when you didn't plan. Always be ready to obey Him. Often it is after you obey that you discover why He wanted you to fast. In January 2012 we were fasting and praying for 7 days with my church members. We were to break the fast every evening but after two days the Holy Spirit told me not to eat and to remain indoors and pray. As I obeyed the heavens were opened over my life. I heard the voice of God very clearly telling me about the future of my ministry and instructions on how I should live my life. After that encounter my ministry moved to another level.

Chapter 3

HOW TO DELIVER YOURSELF

The material in this chapter has been put together to help you pray for your own deliverance. This might not be a complete set of instructions that will work for everybody. In the case where you need to be freed from complicated bondages, do well to consult a true deliverance minister. I say "true deliverance minister" because nowadays there are many fake prophets who are trying to deliver people in the name of Jesus Christ whom they do not know like the sons of Sceva (Acts 19:13-16). Flee away from such men and women.

Self-deliverance is very helpful in many situations where a deliverance minister isn't available to minister to you, and you can be set free from many bondages simply by running yourself through a self-deliverance. However, it can be limited if compared to a regular deliverance session.

If you have been actively involved in occultism, witchcraft or Satanism, it is better that you meet an experienced deliverance minister to help you out because the demons encountered in those situations are usually much stronger, and are best off handled by somebody else. In the course of your personal deliverance session if you begin to feel like you are losing control over yourself and you cannot handle the demons, stop and seek help from an experienced deliverance minister.

STEPS TO SELF-DELIVERANCE

1. Preparing for Self-deliverance

Try to find out the root cause of the problem. You can find out the root cause of your problem by prayer and investigation. Pray and ask the Holy Spirit to show you what the roots to the problem are, and what needs to be done. Pray for His continual guidance and strength during the deliverance session. It is often helpful to ask God to send angels to assist in the deliverance. They can play a powerful role in helping you flush the demons out.

Use the questionnaire I have prepared to check your life. Note down the areas you need to pray about. These include: sins you have to confess; covenants you have to renounce; satanic property you have to destroy; particular evil spirits you have to bind and practical steps you have to take for a changed life. After noting those areas, use this book or my other book *"Power Must Change Hands Vol.1: Dealing with Evil Foundations"* to pray. The first thing you must do before you pray is that you have to read the short teaching concerning that particular area you are dealing with. For example, if you find out that you have a problem with evil dreams, go to *"Power Must Change Hands Vol.1: Dealing with Evil Foundations"* and read the chapter on evil dreams. After reading, use the prayer points at the end of the chapter to carry out your self-deliverance.

2. Warning to non-believers

Deliverance is for believers (Matthew 15:22-28), and is not fit for unbelievers (those who are outside the covenant). If you aren't a born-again Christian, don't even attempt deliverance, because it's like stirring up a bee hive. First accept Jesus Christ as your personal Lord and Savior, and then seek deliverance. This way, you can prevent the demons from returning with several more even worse evil spirits as Jesus warns in Matthew 12:43-45. If you aren't a believer, I wouldn't even try to cast a demon out of anybody. Acts 19:13-16 reveals to us the danger of trying to cast out demons if you aren't true a child of God. The sons of Sceva did not have authority in Jesus because they were unbelievers and 7 men got thrown out of the house naked and beaten by the demon. As you can see, it's not wise or safe to attempt deliverance without Jesus in your life.

3. Prayer and fasting

Prayer and fasting always helps in preparing you for deliverance. Jesus said that some kinds of demons will only come out through prayer and fasting (Mat.17:21). Prayer and fasting builds your faith to the higher levels that is required to cast some demons out. So set aside time to fast before you start to pray for your deliverance.

4. Knowing what is rightfully yours

If you don't believe what is rightfully yours, it's going to be hard to claim it. Your deliverance is first of all tight to what you know. It is after you know that you can exercise your authority over demons. Some of the things you need to know are: you need to understand who you are in Christ; you need to know that your sins are forgiven; you need to have a correct perception of God and your relationship with Him; and you need to know the authority you have been given by God over the enemy. As long as you are a believer you have the authority whether your feel it or not. Mark 16:17 tells us that them who believe will be casting out demons in His name.

5. Find the open doors and break off any legal grounds

I believe this is one of the most important parts of the deliverance process. It is important to find out what opened the door to the enemy, so that we can close it and void their legal right to bother us. There are a number of ways he can gain access, through sins, ancestral sins (which causes ancestral curses), unforgiving heart (which blocks God's forgiveness toward us), dabbling in the occult, demonic vows, fear, etc.

6. Identify the areas of bondage in your life

It is important to know what areas of your life are in bondage. Make a list of the things you want to be freed from. Know exactly what you want to be set free from. Then try to identify the 'open door' that allowed the enemy to move into that area of your life. When did it start? If you had it your entire life, and your parents or grandparents struggled with the same or similar problem, then it was likely generational. Often you can locate what opened up the bondage, if you look back around the time in your life when it started. It's always a good idea to become familiar with the various ways the enemy can gain access into our lives. A good understanding of Legal Rights and Strongholds is always helpful. See the Deliverance Questionnaire.

7. Casting the demons out

Take authority over the demon spirits within you by issuing a command such as, "In the name of Jesus, I now take authority over every evil spirit present within me, and I command each and every one to submit to the authority invested in me by Jesus Christ!"

If you can address the demons by name (lust, anger, suicide, hate, fear, etc.) you will often find them submitting to your authority easier because it makes it harder on them ignore you as if you weren't talking to them. If somebody yelled "hey you!" in a crowd, you probably wouldn't pay any attention to them, but if they yelled out your name, you would be a lot quicker to respond. The same is true with demons, if you address them by name, they are a lot easier to get their attention. Notice how many times Jesus addressed the demons by name, such as deaf and dumb spirits, etc. You can easily identify demons by their manifestations but even if you cannot identify their names, still pray with authority and they will go.

8. Dealing with Demonic Re-enforcements

Demons often work in teams, and if you identify the strongman, it will help you in figuring out their strategies. Once you identify and cast out the strongman, the others go away easily.

Since demons communicate with other demons both within and outside, always forbid and shut down their communication between each other. Command their communicating networks to shut down in Jesus' name.

9. Binding and loosing

Binding is a temporary spiritual handcuffing. If you get worn out and need to continue deliverance the next day, you could simply bind (hand cuff) the remaining demons, and continue the deliverance later on. Binding is also helpful when ministering to somebody else. You can also bind and forbid the demons to interfere with the person as you work with them to tear down strongholds, break up legal grounds, etc.

Loosing is referring to liberating a captive from bondage. Jesus loosed the woman from a spirit of infirmity in Luke 13:12. You might say something like, "I loose myself from the spirit of fear in the name of Jesus! Spirit of fear, I command you to COME OUT in the name of Jesus!"

10. Checking to see if you are free

You should feel a noticeable relief when the demon(s) have left. However, they may just be hiding, and trying to trick you into calling it a success, only to show up their ugly heads later on.

Pray and ask the Holy Spirit to reveal to you if there are any demons remaining that need to be cast out, or whether the deliverance was successful. The long-term effect after a deliverance is usually your best indicator, but when there have been symptoms of the demon (such as fear, anger, suicidal urges, etc.), then I would expect those to be gone when the deliverance has been successful.

Don't also forget to consider that in many cases, deliverance is a process and not just one session. If strongholds need to be torn down that the demons are hanging onto, they can usually take time as you tear them down.

11. Post deliverance instructions

Don't walk in constant fear of demons returning. I also advise you not to play again with the things which opened you up to demons in the first place. Keep your relationship with God cultivated, and don't let the enemy tempt you to let him back in.

Chapter 4

HOW TO FIND A QUALIFIED DELIVERANCE MINISTER

1. Identify a balanced minister

If a minister is very quick to say that all your problems are demonic, without knowing anything about your situation, then you should be careful with such a person. Some people see a demon under every rock, but I am careful not to blame everything on demons. Not all problems are caused by demons. Go to a minister who would take time to find out what your problem really is.

2. A knowledgeable minister

Identify a minister who is knowledgeable. A good deliverance minister should be well-informed and should minister in three main areas: Strongholds (tearing down incorrect thinking patterns), legal grounds (taking away the enemy's right to torment you) and then the casting out part (which requires faith and is exercised by commanding the demons to come out). There are fake deliverance ministers who subdue those who need deliverance to extra-biblical practices. Some people who went for deliverance have been abused by such false prophets. How can you a woman allow a man who is not your husband to anoint your "private parts?" I warn you to be careful with such individuals. You can end up with more demons rather than being delivered. Refuse to do anything that is not recorded in the Bible and run away with your soul.

3. A Minister who Ministers in Love and Compassion

Some people have actually felt hurt by people in the deliverance ministry. One reason for this is because some people simply do not minister in love and compassion, and end up creating unnecessary fears that are based on lies and false teachings. If you can identify someone who can minister to you with love and compassion, it is the best.

4. Run Away from Fear-driven ministries

One thing that you should watch out for, is fear-driven ministries. I call them fear-driven, because they often put a lot of fear into people that is NOT from God, and is completely unnecessary. They don't show you the love of Christ and build you up, they spend time talking to you about the devil and demons. Some people have been delivered from demonization and have come under the manipulation of ungodly ministers. I once helped a Christian sister who spent time reading only books on demonology and spiritual warfare. She was filled with a lot of fear. I ceased all those books from her and directed her to read other books that could build up her faith. All the scaring dreams she was having vanished away. Today she is very fine in the faith.

After deliverance, you have to go on to enjoy the freedom Christ has made available for you. In this book I have tried to strike a balance so that you do not remain a perpetual captive in your mind. Do not allow anyone to keep you in bondage through any means.

Chapter 5

DELIVERANCE QUESTIONNAIRE

This questionnaire will help any deliverance minister or any individual who desires to carry out his deliverance. The questions will help you to discern the different bondages that you need to deal with. The questions can reveal strongholds, demonic bondages and legal grounds that may need to be addressed as you pray. Answer the questions on a piece of paper then use them during your prayer session.

Part I: The bondage

1. When did this bondage start?
2. Was there any unusual things that took place (or you did) when this bondage started?

3. If this bondage started when you were a child: Do you have ancestors who have suffered from a similar kind of bondage?
4. What kind of bondage are you facing? (Fears, depression, voices in your mind, mental illness, physical illness, mental torment, spiritual torment, etc. Please be as detailed as possible.)
5. What are all the things that have impacted your life? (Parent's death, trauma, a certain situation that changed your life, anything that 'changed' you.)

Part II: Your ancestor's background

1. Do you have ancestors who have struggled with similar problems or bondages?
2. Did your bondage start as a child and appear to have no reason to be there?
3. Do you have siblings who suffer from similar bondages or oppression?

Part III: Soul ties

1. Have you been involved with extramarital sex? Are you attracted to an ex-lover? Is he or she a good/godly influence for you?
2. Have you been divorced?

3. Do you feel an unusual attraction to a past boyfriend, girlfriend or lover (who is obviously not right for you)?
4. Do you let anybody dominate, control, or make your choices you?
5. Have you ever formed a blood covenant with another person? (Blood brothers, etc.)
6. Have you ever made vows or agreements with somebody in effort to strengthen the relationship or commit yourself to each other?
7. Do you see any ungodly relationships in your past where gifts were exchanged? (Are you holding onto something that was given to you from somebody you had adultery with, etc.)
8. Have you ever had ungodly sexual relations with animals?
9. Do you have any pictures in your possession of somebody whom you may have an ungodly soul tie with? (A picture of you with somebody you had an adultery with, etc.)

Part IV: Relationship with parents

1. What do you think of your parents?
2. How would you explain your childhood?
3. Where you close to your parents while growing up? If not, why?
4. How would you explain your relationship with your parents? Was it good, bad or very cold?

5. Did you feel rejection from your parents?
6. Was either of your parents overly passive or controlling?
7. Has either of your parents been divorced? Remarried? Are your parents divorced?
8. How would you describe your relationship with your siblings growing up?

Part V: Rejection and abuse

1. Were your parents married when you were conceived? Were you the right sex? Did your parents not want you, or want you to be different (gender, etc.) in any way? If so, explain.
2. Did you feel rejected as a child? As an adult? If so, by whom? Explain.
3. Did you face abuse? What kind (emotional, physical, sexual, etc.) and by whom?
4. Have you faced rejection from your peers, classmates, friends or those around you?
5. Have you ever been put down, belittled, or made fun of? If so, by whom? Explain.
6. If you have faced rejection or abuse, how did you respond? Do you feel you are still paying a price for it? If so, how?
7. How do you respond to rejection right now?
8. Do you reject yourself (self-rejection)? If so, why and in what ways?

Part VI: Unforgiveness or bitterness

1. Is there anybody you feel edgy around? (Don't like them, feel anything in your heart against them, etc.)
2. Do you have anything against anybody? In other words, is there anybody that you have a hard time demonstrating the love of Christ to?
3. Has anybody wronged you that you haven't forgiven from your heart (thoughts, feelings, emotions, etc.)?
4. How do your view your siblings, parents, co-workers, etc.? Do you have any hard feelings against them?
5. Do you make a habit of blaming yourself for everything? Do you obsess over your mistakes and feel unusually guilty for them?
6. Do you deeply regret things that you've done in your past? Could you kick yourself over something you've done in your past? If so, explain.

Part VII: Personality

1. Are you a very positive or negative person?
2. Do you feel confident in yourself? If so, why?
3. Do you have a low self-esteem? If so, why?

4. Are you domineering or controlling? If so, to whom, and in what ways? Why?
5. Are you an achiever? (A go-getter) If so, in what ways?
6. Do you feel that you are always right and that if everybody did everything your way, this world would be a better place to live?
7. How do you treat your children? Husband? Are you controlling, passive, etc.?
8. Do you like people to 'look at you' (as in receive attention)?

Part VIII: Emotional health

1. Do you strive to feel accepted? If so, how does this affect your lifestyle? By whom do you want to feel accepted?
2. Are you always stressed out? If so, why?
3. Do you feel hurt? If so, by whom/what and why?
4. Do you feel good about yourself? If not, why?
5. Do you feel depressed? If so, why? When did it start? Did your parents or grandparents struggle with depression? If so, then do you know when it started and why? Do you have siblings who are also struggling? Do you feel your depression is rational or irrational?

6. Do you struggle with fears? If so, what is it that you fear? (Fear of heights, dying, being hopeless, failure, never marrying, etc.)

7. Do you worry about things? What things do you worry about? Why?

8. Do you struggle with anger? Do you have a short temper?

9. Do you have any insecurities? If so, explain.

10. Do you feel any self-pity or feel sorry for yourself?
Have you ever felt this? If so, why?

11. Do you find it easy to hate people? If so, over what kinds of things would a person have to do to make you hate them?

12. Do you have any irrational feelings? If so, what are they?

13. Do you feel like something is wrong with you?

14. Do you feel excessively guilty over anything? Is this a continual problem?

15. Are you very confused and forgetful? (Beyond the normal)

16. Are you aware of any emotional wounds that have affected you?

17. Have you ever been deeply embarrassed over something? What was it?

18. Have you been in or are currently experiencing very difficult (depressing) circumstances which may cause you to feel hopeless or depressed?

Part IX: Who are you in Christ? And how do you see God?

1. How do you explain your relationship with God?
2. Do you feel you aren't good enough to meet His standards?
3. Do you see Him as a loving father, or
   1. a dictator?
4. Do you believe that it's only by the Blood of Jesus that your sins are forgiven? Or do you feel you need to earn your forgiveness in any way?
5. Do you feel God's love in your life?
6. Do you feel like your sins are forgiven? Or do you feel guilty?
7. Do you feel excessively guilty in everyday life?
8. Do you feel that doing good things, you earn God's love and acceptance?
9. Do you feel that God is angry or upset with you?

Part X: Spoken curses, vows & oaths

1. Have you ever spoken something negative about yourself that has came to past? For example: "I'm sick and tired..." or "If I don't quit typing, I'm going to get arthritis!"
2. Has your parents, or those in authority over you spoken out a curse over you? For example: "You'll

never amount to anything!" or "You'll never get out of debt" or "You're so dumb"

3. Have you ever made a vow out of anger? If so, what? For example: "I'll never let anybody push me around again!" or "I'm never going to be hurt again!"

4. Have you ever wished to die? Have you ever said it?

5. If you have made any vows or oaths, what are they?

Part XI: Relationships

1. Do you have many friends? What kind of people are they?

2. Do you have a hard time trying to meet new people or make friends?

3. Are you socially outgoing or shy? If so, why?

4. How would you define your relationship with your spouse?

Part XII: Sexuality

1. Have you ever had unholy sex? What kind? (Fornication, adultery, sodomy, bestiality, with a child, etc.)

2. Have you struggled with lust, fantasy or unholy sexual thoughts? If so, what kind?

3. Have you been attracted to pornography?

4. Do you have homosexual thoughts and desires? If so, have you acted upon those feelings?

5. How do you feel about your sexuality? (Do you feel dirty about it, or do you feel it's a wonderful blessing that God's given you?)

6. Do you withhold sex from your spouse or are you fidgety? Do you enjoy a healthy relationship with your spouse sexually? How does he or she react?

7. Have you ever been raped or sexually abused?

8. Have you ever woke up and felt a sexual presence with you? There are demons that imitate male and female functions, and stimulate their host (a person) sexually (beyond the normal 'wet dream').

9. Do you struggle or have you struggled with masturbation?

10. Do you struggle or have you struggled with any other sexual related thoughts, desires, or bondages?

11. Is there anything sexually that you are ashamed of?

Part XIII: Addictions

1. Do you have any addictions? If so, what kind? (Drugs, alcohol, smoking, eating, sex, TV, etc.) When did they start?

2. Did anybody else in your family (siblings, ancestors, etc.) have a struggle with any addictions? If so, what? Who?
3. Have you ever had, or currently have any sort of obsession over anything? If so, what?

Part XIV: False religions

Examples of false religions: Buddhism, Hindu, Jehovah Witness, Mormonism, Christian Scientists, eastern religions, etc.

1. Have you ever been involved with any false religions? If so, why, when and how long? How do you feel about those beliefs now?
2. Have you ever been involved in any secret societies such as Freemasonry? If so, how deep were you involved?

Part XV: The occult & Satanism

1. Have you ever shown interest in the occult? If so, in what ways? (Read up on it, dabbled in it, etc.)
2. Do you still feel drawn or attracted to the occult?
3. Have you had any interest in horror or thriller style movies or novels? Are you still attracted to these things?
4. Have you ever made a vow with the devil? If so, what?

5. Married Satan?
6. Worshipped a demon or Satan?
7. Have you ever put a curse or spell on somebody?
8. Are you aware of any curses or spells placed on you? If so, what? Who did it?
9. Dabbled with an Ouija board? If so, why?
10. Ever been a member of a coven (group of 13 witches)?
   Explain.
11. Communicated with the dead? Explain.
12. Told somebody's fortune or went to see a fortune teller? Explain.
13. Ever read your horoscope?
14. Watched or been involved in a séance? Explain.
15. Been involved or a victim of Satanic Ritual Abuse (SRA)? Explain.
16. Been baptized into a false religion or any other evil baptism? If so, what were you baptized into? When?
17. Have you ever had a spirit guide?
18. Have you ever been involved with meditation, yoga, karate, or related activities?
19. Were you or anybody in your family superstitious? If so, who?
20. Ever been involved in astral travel? (Out of body)
21. If you have made any vows or oaths, what are they? Were there any sacrifices or rituals that was accompanied with them?

22. Have you ever made a blood pact before? If so, with whom (including persons, demons and Satan) and for what purpose?
23. Have you ever partaken in automatic writing, automatic drawing or automatic painting?
24. Have you ever been involved in Yoga, transcendental meditation, or similar activities? So, what happened? How did it affect you?

Part XIX: Weaknesses

1. Do you struggle with any habitual sins? If so, what? Do you want to break those bad habits?
2. Do you struggle with any weaknesses such as lust, anger, hate, etc.? If so, what? Do you know where they came from or how they got started? Do you want to break free from those weaknesses?

Part XX: Pregnancy issues

1. Have you ever said something along the lines of, "I will never have children"?
2. Have you ever had an abortion or attempted one?
3. Have you ever had incest or ungodly sexual relations with somebody related to you? (See Leviticus 20:19-21, as this can cause a curse to land upon you which needs to be broken)

Part XXI: Other things to look for

1. Have you ever tried drugs? If so, how much, and how did it affect you? Why did you try drugs?
2. Have you ever thought about or attempted suicide?
3. Do you have any physical or mental disabilities, diseases or illnesses? Explain.
4. Do you want, and are willing to be delivered? Are you willing to give up those demon spirits and maybe make some lifestyle changes in order to keep your deliverance?
5. Do you experience unusual confusion settle upon you as you try to pray and read the Bible?
6. What kind of music do you like? (Please list all styles of music you currently enjoy, and give

examples in each category you list, such as some names of artists and songs)

7. Have you previously enjoyed ndombolo, mapouka, coupe decale, hard rock, metal, acid, alternative, rap, new age, or any other kind of worldly music? (Please provide some examples of artists and songs from each genre (type/style) of music you list).

8. Have you had any nightmares or weird experiences at night while supposedly sleeping?

9. Have you ever been in a trance or had an out of body experience?

10. Have you ever noticed time slipped right out from under you? For example, you look at your watch and it's 7:00pm, then you look again what seemed like 15 minutes later and it's 2:00am. This is a sign of a trance.

11. Have you ever touched or kissed a dead body? If so, explain whom and why and what happened afterwards.

12. Do you feel that you somehow have to earn your forgiveness? Do you 'wonder' if your sins are truly forgiven -- all of them? Are you aware of any signs of legalism or religious spirits operating in your mind?

13. Do you have any physical infirmities, sickness or diseases? If so, please list them.

14. Are you on any medications? If so, please explain.
15. Have you ever had any other kind of weird encounter with the spiritual realm?

Part 2:

PRAYER

MARATHON

Chapter 6

PROPHETIC DECLARATIONS OVER YOUR LIFE

1. *By the power of the resurrection of our Lord Jesus Christ, I speak life to dead things in my life, in the name of Jesus.*

2. *By the power of the resurrection of our Lord Jesus Christ, let me be catapulted to the level my enemies says I will not reach, in the name of Jesus.*

3. *I shall have unstoppable advancement from today in Jesus' Name.*

4. *This year, treasures of dark places shall be transferred to my bosom, in Jesus' Name.*

5. *This year, my star shall arise and shall fall no more, in Jesus' Name.*

6. *This year, men shall chase me around with blessings, in Jesus Name.*

7. *I recover ten-fold all my wasted years, in Jesus' Name.*

8. *This year, men shall compete to favor me, in Jesus' Name*

9. *The works of my hands shall be favored in the name of Jesus.*

10. *All the days of my life, I shall be a wonder to unbelievers in the name of Jesus.*

11. *I take charge of the heavenlies and I declare that it shall be well with me, my family, my church and my nation in the name of Jesus.*

12. *O ye doors of promotion and favour, open for me, in the name of Jesus.*

13. *By the power of the Holy Spirit I will move from the minimum level of life to the maximum.*

14. *Goodness and mercy shall follow me all the days of my life in the name of Jesus.*

15. *I declare open every closed door in my life in Jesus' name.*

16. *By the mercy of God, every scarcity in my life shall turn to abundance in Jesus' name.*

17. *From today no devil shall put a yoke on me again in Jesus' name.*

18. *In the mighty name of Jesus the power of God shall always shield me and overshadow me.*

19. *In the mighty name of Jesus, I shall fulfill my divine destiny.*

20. *In the mighty name of Jesus, I shall leave a legacy for my descendants.*

21. *I shall not die before time in the name of Jesus.*

DAY 1:

CONSECRATION

Bible Reading: *Psalm 51, 1Samuel 1: 1-17*

The Hebrew word *"qadash"* means to be clean, to dedicate, to be holy, to purify, and to sanctify. In simple terms consecration means to dedicate something or somebody for a particular purpose. Under the Old Testament the priests and all those who wanted to meet God had to obligatorily perform some consecration rituals. These rituals dealt with the individual's sins and also prepared the person to meet God. In 1Samuel 1:1-17 we see the people of Israel gathered to seek God in fasting at Mizpeh. While they were consecrating themselves and praying before God, the Philistines came as usual to attack them. This time this turned around in favor of Israel. God thundered from heaven that day and devoured their enemies. This is what will happen as you consecrate yourself to seek God in this season.

"The LORD will fight for you, and you shall hold your peace." (Exo.14:14).

Put Your Heart in Order

"Then you will call upon Me and go and pray to Me, and I will listen to you. And you will seek Me and find Me, when you search for Me with all your heart." (Jer.29: 12-13)

The condition of your heart will determine the effectiveness of your prayer. There are things in your life that God does not like and you might not even know. If you really desire to meet God in this season, confess and turn away from the sins you know. If you refuse to deal with your sins and you go on to fast and pray, God will not hear you. Your prayer and fasting will be wasted labor.

"If I had known of any sin in my heart, the Lord would not have listened to me." (Ps.66:18) NCV

Also pray and ask the Holy Spirit to search and expose to you the evil that is hidden in your heart that you do not know. Pray like David;

"Search me, O God, and know my heart: try me, and know my thoughts: And see if there be any wicked way in me, and lead me in the way everlasting." (Ps.139:2324).

One other thing about your heart is that it can be focused on other things when your mouth is praying. During this season of prayer, the Lord is saying emphatically,

"pray to Me, and I will listen to you. And you will seek Me and find Me, when you search for Me with all your heart." (Jer.29: 12-13).

I therefore encourage you to seek God with all your heart. Refuse to let anything cheat you by distracting you.

The Anointing of Prayer

When Jesus' disciples came to Him and requested that He should teach them how to pray, I thought He would rebuke them (Luke11:1-10). He didn't rebuke them but took time to teach them because we ought to be taught how to pray effectively. Not only do we need to be taught to pray, we also need an anointing to pray effectively.

"Shall I bring to the point of birth and then not deliver?" asks the Lord your God. "No! Never!" (Isa.66:9) TLB

It is actually God who impregnates a person with the burden for prayer and also the ability to pray through. Until this happens to you, it is difficult to really experience power in prayer. I am convinced that this anointing of prayer is coming on you today as you ask God to release it on your life. He will put the right burden on your heart and He will also empower you to pray so effectively that there will be mighty testimonies.

Dedicate Your Whole Life

In order to encounter God during this season of prayer your spiritual senses have to be alive. Let me say that you need "a spiritual network."
"Now we have received, not the spirit of the world, but the spirit which is of God; that we might know the things that are freely given to us of God." (1Cor.2:12).

There are many things concerning your life, family and destiny that you need to know. The Lord has made it possible for you to even see into your future by the power of the Holy Spirit. So ask for the anointing of the Holy Spirit on your spiritual senses to enable you enter into contact with the deep things of God concerning you.

PRAYER POINTS

1. *Worship and thank God for your life, family, the church and the nation.*

2. *Dear Holy Spirit search my heart and expose every evil hidden in me.*

3. *Lord forgive me of my sins (mention those you know).*

4. *Lord, forgive and cleanse me of all the sins I do not know.*

5. *Seek the forgiveness and mercy of God for your family, the church and the nation.*

6. *Lord, blot away my iniquity and wipe away guilt from my life.*

7. *Lord, deliver me from every root of inherited sin in Jesus' name.*

8. *Lord, purge my life with the blood of Jesus Christ.*

9. *Lord, open the doors of your presence to me.*

10. *O Lord, Fill me with the spirit of brokenness and holiness.*

11. *Lord, give me a pure heart and the fear of God.*

12. *Let every filthy garment in my life burn to ashes in Jesus' name.*

13. *Let every power of defilement in my life receive fire in Jesus' name.*

14. *I bind and overpower every anti-holiness spirit in my life in Jesus' name.*

15. *Let the fire of the Holy Ghost purge my eyes, my ears, and my entire life.*

16. *I receive the garment of holiness over my life in Jesus' name.*

17. *I receive the garment of fire in Jesus' name.*

18. *I welcome the anointing on spiritual eyes, ears, and senses.*

19. *O Lord, baptize me with the anointing of fervent and effective prayer.*

20. *Let every hidden secret I am supposed to know concerning my destiny manifest in Jesus' name.*

21. *Let every mystery of wickedness working against my life be exposed by fire.*

22. *I receive understanding of every revelation God is giving me in this season in Jesus' name.*

23. *I recover all my lost dreams in Jesus' name.*

24. *I expose every evil plans of the devil against my life in Jesus' name.*

25. *Let the fire of the Holy Ghost fall upon my family for revival in Jesus' name.*

26. *Let the fire of God fall in my church and expose the works of the enemy.*

27. *Lord, raise and sustain apostles, prophets, evangelists, pastors and teachers who will stir a revival in this nation.*

DAYS 2-3:
PURSUE, OVERTAKE AND RECOVER ALL

Bible Reading: *1Samuel 30:1-26, 2Kings 6:1-7*

I want us to start by defining some few terms:

Pursue: means to chase after, to hunt, to advance, participate, to search for and pursue with hostile intent, to catch or capture something with persistence.

Overtake: means to catch up with and pass a person moving in the same direction, to reach and then surpass a level achieved by somebody, to come over somebody suddenly, to catch somebody by surprise, to achieve a level once obtained that you've lost and not only catch up but to pass it and take it by surprise.

Recover all means: to deliver, to rescue, to defend, to pluck, to regain as in former condition, to recover anew, and to regain one's position.
This is the time to catch up, to redeem the time, and to overtake.

What Have You Lost?

People only go out on risky recovery missions when they have lost something, they consider to be very value. You would agree with me that you have lost certain things that you didn't even bother to go looking for them. Infact when some people lost certain things, they have a sense of relief instead because those things had become burdensome to them. A man like David will not be quiet when his wives, children and property have been taken away by the enemy.

There also people who have lost some valuable spiritual or physical blessings but who are not bothered about them. Until you are disturbed God will not do anything. It is only when David went to God and asked what he should do that God told him to "pursue, overtake and recover all". Had it been that he continued to cry like his friends the enemies could have gone with their families and property for good.

Personal level

There are things you have lost personally. It could be that you have lost the anointing and your spiritual life has become a caricature of the fiery man of God or woman of God you used to be. It maybe you are still a believer in Christ but you have lost your spiritual gifts. Could it be that you have lost your health? Your own could be that you have lost your marriage; your spouse has been seized by a certain strange man or woman. It maybe you are chaffing in lack because you have lost your job? For some, they keep missing important opportunities to move to the next level in life. What have you lost that must be recovered? Let me ask you this last question concerning your life; "are you where God intended you to be right now?"

Family level

Each family has a special place in God's global plan of salvation and the restoration of human dignity. This is your family inheritance in God. In the Bible the family of Aaron was chosen to be God's priests (Exo.19:6). The family of Levi was selected among the twelve tribes of Israel to be God's servants (Num.1:50). The family of Asaph was chosen to be musicians in the temple of the Lord (1Chron.25:6). Each of the twelve tribes of Israel had a specific assignment to fulfill. The leadership scepter was given to the tribe of Judah.

Your family has a special place in God's plan. The question is "are you fulfilling this divine plan?" Some families are noted today as thieves, prostitutes, criminals, chronic idol worshippers, witchdoctors, sorcerers, wicked people, etc. God did not raise any family to produce armed robbers or criminals. The truth is that Satan has stolen something from these families and has planted an evil seed. Some families are very gifted but the devil has corrupted the gifts. For example, we have some families that have good singers but Satan has corrupted them to become ungodly musicians that are polluting many and leading them to hell. Some families are very gifted in business but they do terrible types businesses to raise money. You must ask God to help you identify the gifts and blessings He has ordained for your family so that you can pray for their manifestation. As long as the devil is in control the gifts will not manifest.

God has given each family a man or a woman who is supposed to be a channel for the different blessings that family needs. It maybe you are crying for a pastor for your family when the pastor God gave you is still a drunkard somewhere. It maybe you are asking God why he has forgotten your family while the Joseph who will supply the needs of your family is still in prison. You must pray for divine recovery and manifestation. Hold God to open a new page for your family.

National level

Each nation (ethnic group or country) just like the families has a special place in God's global plan of salvation. The strategy of the devil is to raise the wrong people to positions of power so as to mislead the people. As God's people we all have to find out the blessings Satan has stolen from us and begin to cry out to God for restoration. The nation of Cameroon is so reach in natural resources but at the same time very poor. The problem is that the wrong people are in control. Satan has polluted the minds of the people with fear so they embezzle public funds to secure a better tomorrow for themselves and their families. We must pray for the recovery of the lost blessings of our nation.

At this time, you have to prayerfully examine your life, your family, your church and the nation to find out the blessings that have been stolen by the enemy. When you must have identified them, write them down and start to pray for total recovery. Set your mind to pray until something happens. Many lives, families, churches and communities are lying in ruin because nobody has prayed for their restoration. If you decide to pray from today, within the next few years a new story will be reported about you, your family, your church and your community.

PRAYER POINTS

1. *Take time and worship God for bringing you to this special season of divine recovery.*
2. *Thank God because He is going to restore lost blessings in your life.*
3. *O Lord, forgive me for any carelessness that has given the devil the opportunity to steal from me in the name of Jesus.*
4. *Lord, forgive me for mismanaging the resources you gave me in the name of Jesus.*
5. *Lord, forgive me for following the evil and sinful ways of my parents in the name of Jesus.*
6. *Lord, forgive my church and community for opening up to demons through sin.*
7. *O Lord God of mercy, have mercy upon us and release the river of restoration to heal us and our land.*
8. *Let the fire of the Holy Spirit purge me from spiritual slumber, negligence and carelessness.*
9. *O Lord, release the fire of the Holy Ghost upon my life for total recovery in my life and family in the name of Jesus.*

10. *Lord, put a passion in my heart and cause me not to rest until I become what you want me to be in the name of Jesus.*

11. *Lord, open my eyes to discover my divine inheritance, as well as the stolen blessings of my family in the name of Jesus.*

12. *Lord, open the eyes of church leaders to discover the blessings that the devil has stolen from the church in the name of Jesus.*

13. *In the mighty name of Jesus, I stand today on the finished work of the cross and I cancel any covenant established by my forefathers and evil spirits that mortgaged the blessings of my family with the blood of Jesus.*

14. *In the mighty name of Jesus, I cancel any satanic record that gives evil spirits the right to hold my family blessings in the name of Jesus.*

15. *In the mighty name of Jesus, I use the blood of Jesus to cancel any satanic legal ground that permits the devil to oppress our church in the name of Jesus.*

16. *In the mighty name of Jesus, I use the blood of Jesus to cancel any satanic legal ground that permits the devil to imprison the blessings of our nation in the name of Jesus.*

17. *I bind any spiritual strongman responsible for keeping me and my family away from our blessings in the name of Jesus.*

18. I command any demonic power sitting over my divine inheritance to scatter by fire in the name of Jesus.

19. In the mighty name of Jesus, I command all the force of darkness sitting over the blessings of my tribe to scatter by fire.

20. I the mighty name of Jesus, I command all the forces of darkness manipulating the blessings of this nation to scatter by fire.

21. O Lord, let your east wind blow through my life, family, church and nation for a mighty breakthrough.

22. My Father, Let the river of divine restoration bring salvation, healing, deliverance and breakthrough into my life, family, church and nation in the name of Jesus.

23. Lord, raise anointed men and women of in each family in this nation.

DAYS 4-5:
ANOINTING FOR TOTAL RECOVERY

Bible Reading: *1Samuel 30:1-26, 2Kings 6:1-7*

Anything Lost Can Be Recovered

David and his men had lost all their families and all possessions when he returned to Ziklag. In order to render the situation very hopeless the enemies had burnt down all the houses to ashes. (1Sam.30:1-3). From man's point of view it was a hopeless case but from God's perspective total recovery was very possible.

"So David inquired of the LORD, saying, "Shall I pursue this troop? Shall I overtake them?" And He answered him, "Pursue, for you shall surely overtake them and without fail recover all." (1Sam.30:8).

Anything you have lost on this planet can be recovered when the hand of God is released on your behalf. Our God is the Almighty God who has everything under His control. He is Omniscient which means He sees everything everywhere at every time. In this season this God is in a mission of divine recovery in your life. His anointing will come on your life for the impossible to become possible.

The Laws of Divine Restoration

1. The law of double recovery
"If a man delivers to his neighbor money or articles to keep, and it is stolen out of the man's house, if the thief is found, he shall pay double." (Exo.22:7).

"People do not despise a thief If he steals to satisfy himself when he is starving. Yet when he is found, he must restore sevenfold; He may have to give up all the substance of his house." (Prov.6:30-31).

One of the ways by which people lost things in this life is theft. The Bible calls the devil a thief who comes to steal, kill and destroy (John 10:10). The interesting thing is that God has instituted a law for the restoration of stolen things. When David and his men caught up with their enemies, they recovered all they had lost and even more (1Sam.30:19). God gave them bonus because He was pleased with David. As you rise up in prayer in this season the forces of destruction that have been stealing from your life will be arrested by fire. Just as heaven has

88

sanctioned that your recovery should be doublefold, you will not only get back what you have lost, it shall come back double.

2. The law of divine exposition
"For there is nothing covered that will not be revealed, nor hidden that will not be known." (Luke 12:2).

Many things have been lost because the enemy has hidden them. Sometimes the enemy succeeds to cast a veil over the good things God has released into our lives. There are Christians who are loaded with great spiritual gifts that are meant to impact this generation but the enemy in one way of the other has kept them in spiritual obscurity. Some people are sitting on great treasures but they are blind to them. In this season the schemes of the devil behind your predicaments will be exposed by fire. Those who are zealously serving the devil like Saul of Tarsus will receive divine light for destiny recovery. Anyone that has been forgotten in prison like Joseph will be brought to the lime light.

3. The law of divine acceleration

There are certain lost things that can only be recovered supernaturally.

"Then David said to him, "To whom do you belong, and where are you from?" And he said, "I am a young man from Egypt, servant of an Amalekite; and my master left me behind, because three days ago I fell sick." (1Sam.30:13).

David and his men were trying to rescue their families and property from aggressive Amalekites who had seized them more than three days earlier. One other challenge was that they did not know the exact direction these enemies took. Though it seemed an impossible mission, God gave them divine speed to overtake the enemies. While they were pursuing fast, God caused the enemies to settle down and begin to celebrate. It may be you are in a situation that people call "lateness in life," My God will give you a divine push. That yoke of delay over your life and family is broken in Jesus' name. You will use a shorter time to get what took others many years to get. Any condition in your life, family, ministry and in our nation that has stagnated is going to shoot forward again.

4. The law of resurrection
"Jesus said to her, "I am the resurrection and the life. He who believes in Me, though he may die, he shall live." (John 11:25).

Certain things are lost when the power of death invades one's life. In those days when a city was captured and burnt to ashes, those taken captive were considered dead. Only a miracle could bring them to their original state. For David and his men to have recovered their families it was a picture of resurrection. In the season of restoration God releases the power of resurrection to bring back dead things to life. This anointing is coming on you as you pray this month. Spiritual gifts that have died in your life are coming back to life again because Jesus Christ – the Resurrection and the Life is stepping in a new way. Dead businesses, marriage, relationships, etc. are coming back to life.

5. The law of divine attraction

"So the man of God said, "Where did it fall?" And he showed him the place. So he cut off a stick, and threw it in there; and he made the iron float." (2Kings 6:6).

Certain precious things are lost by accident – unexpected. This is what happened to the borrowed axe the sons of the prophets were using for their building project. The axe-head came out and fell into the River Jordan. The question they should have been asking was, "where do we begin?" It was not going to be easy to retrieve it. Thank God the man of God Elisha was around. When he came around, God revealed to him the law of divine attraction. He cut a stick and threw it in the river. The metallic axe-head was divinely attracted to the stick and he took it and gave to the young prophets.

This miracle reveals that when your time for divine restoration comes lost things are miraculously recovered by the law of attraction. This is what is going to happen to you as you pray in this season. What has been lost, no matter far it has gone will locate you in Jesus' name. Separated couples will come back together by a divine pull. Families that are torn apart will be drawn together so that enemies will become friends again by the power of the Holy Spirit.

Your time to bounce back

In this season God is saying – take back your inheritance, this is a season of new beginnings, of restoration and fresh anointing. This season the Church taking back her lost inheritance that has been stolen like never before – healing is being taken back, worship is being taken back, and evangelism is being taken back. This is also time to rediscover what the devil has stolen from you and your family for many generations. Not only are you going to discover your God-given inheritance, you will take possession of it. How will it happen? The anointing of divine recovery will come on you and the impossible will become possible.

God wants you to know that in spite of what the devil tries to pull down, you can recover all. We must seek to recover all that the devil has sought to take from us. No matter what it is you may have thought you lost, no matter what may have knocked you down, no matter who may have hurt or betrayed you, you have to get up, pursue, overtake, and recover all the blessings that the devil of this world is trying to take from you. You can't give up the fight for your right to thrive and prosper in life because you may have experienced a couple of setbacks. The fight isn't over simply because you've lost a round or two. Your future is full of glorious tomorrows, and your breakthrough is just around the corner

PRAYER POINTS
1. *Take time and worship God for bringing you to this special season of divine recovery.*
2. *Thank God because He is going to restore lost blessings in your life.*

3. *O Lord, forgive me for any carelessness that has given the devil the opportunity to steal from me in the name of Jesus.*

4. *Lord, thank you because you will restore .... (name it) that the devil has stolen in the name of Jesus.*

5. *Take time and pray that God should activate the 5 laws of divine restoration (5 anointings for divine restoration) that I have explained above in your life and family.*

6. *Use the laws to pray for different areas of your life that need divine restoration. For example if you have lost your job and you need another one, pray like this; In the mighty name of Jesus, let the anointing of divine attraction connect men to a new job better than the one I lost.*

7. *I command any satanic army that has taken captive .... (mention names) scatter to pieces in the name of Jesus.*

8. *O Mighty God of King David, send the angels of divine recovery into my life, family and church for miraculous recovery of lost generational blessings in the name of Jesus.*

9. *O Lord, let the anointing of resurrection cause every dead thing in my life and family to come back to life.*

10. *My Father, release the anointing of divine attraction to bring back all I have lost in the name of Jesus.*

11. *O Lord, let the anointing of divine acceleration fall on me today for total recovery.*

12. *My Father, let doors of restoration, salvation, healing, provision, favor, promotion and fruitfulness open in my life, family, church and this nation in the name of Jesus.*

13. *O Lord, cause you wind to blow through my life and cause the good in me to manifest.*

14. *O Lord, let your fire burn every veil that has caused darkness to prevail over any area of my life in the name of Jesus.*

15. *My Father, let your east wind blow through my family and expose every evil that has been ruining us in the name of Jesus.*

16. *O God of mercy, let there be total recovery of everything the devil has stolen from me.*

17. *My Father, according to your word, give me seven fold recovery in this area of my life ……. (name it) in the name of Jesus.*

18. *O God of revival, let lost spiritual gifts, anointing, evangelism, giving, fasting, love and faith be restored in the churches in this nation in the name of Jesus.*

19. *O Lord, let your east wind blow through my life, family, church and nation for a mighty breakthrough.*

20. *My Father, Let the river of divine restoration bring salvation, healing, deliverance and breakthrough into my life, family, church and nation in the name of Jesus.*

21. *O Lord, cause my family to see miracles we have never seen in the name of Jesus.*

DAYS 6-7:
THE POWER OF SACRIFICE

Bible Reading: *John 12: 24-26, Romans 12:1-3*

There is a law that God employs anytime He wants to multiply anything and that law is the law of sacrifice. Whenever the law of sacrifice is set on motion, there is a release of mighty spiritual power. This explains why many demonic rituals involve some kind of sacrifice. Various animals and sometimes human beings are sacrificed in rituals to release power. Occultists make sacrifices. Usually people seeking for spiritual power are asked to make sacrifices. Consider the case of the King of Moab who experienced a mighty turn around in the battle he fought against Edom and Israel after he sacrificed his heir.

"And when the king of Moab saw that the battle was too fierce for him, he took with him seven hundred men who drew swords, to break through to the king of Edom, but they could not. Then he took his eldest son who would have reigned in his place, and offered him as a burnt offering upon the wall; and there was great indignation against

Israel. So they departed from him and returned to their own land." (2Kgs.3:26-27).

The rabbis say that the king of Moab called his notables and tried to find out the secret of Israel's power and was told that it was sacrifice so he too sacrificed his own son to his gods. The power released by the king's sacrifice turned away the approaching armies. The sacrifice saved the king's life and the lives of his people. Sacrifice will always release power. Many pastors and Christians are powerless because they make no sacrifices for the Lord.

What is a sacrifice?

The Advanced Learner's dictionary defines sacrifice this way; "To kill an animal or person and offer to a god or gods"; "To give up something that is valuable to you in order to help another person." The Hebrew word translated as sacrifice in the Old Testament is "*zebach*" which means slaughter; the victim or the act of slaughtering. You see here that sacrificing is very costly because it involves the shedding of blood.

The sacrifice we are talking about here has to do with giving up something that is very valuable to

98

you in order to please our Lord Jesus Christ. This is a key to the release of mighty spiritual power. Fasting, sacrificial giving, going out for missions and serving God acceptably are all examples of spiritual sacrifices. Let me also add here that every ministry God has committed into your hands has sacrifices you must make. Unless you are ready to pay the price, you will never see the expected results. A lot of gimmicks and manipulations are being employed in ministerial circles today because men and women are not ready to pay the required price for the release of power for their ministries.

What are the marks of a true sacrifice?

1. It is offered willing and not by force.
2. It is motivated by deep love and compassion.
3. It is not motivated by gain.
4. It is released without strings.
5. It is costly.
6. It is painful.

Generally, sacrifices are offered by matured people and not babes. It is common to see mothers serve food to their families but sleep hungry. The kids cannot do that. Your level of sacrifice is determined by your level of spiritual maturity. There is a brand of Christianity today that is not biblical. This type of

Christianity only emphasizes the divine prosperity of the Christian. True biblical Christianity teaches that,

"I have been crucified with Christ; it is no longer I who live, but Christ lives in me; and the life which I now live in the flesh I live by faith in the Son of God, who loved me and gave Himself for me." (Gal.2:20).

Biblical Christianity therefore is living to please Jesus Christ first and not yourself. It is as you live to satisfy the will of Jesus Christ that God anoints you and sets you up in the place of dominion in life for the glory of His name.

"You have loved righteousness and hated lawlessness; Therefore God, Your God, has anointed You With the oil of gladness more than Your companions." (Heb.1:9).

It is God's desire that you should grow in the spirit of sacrifice in order to benefit more from the power He has made available for His children. As you continue to seek Him with a humble heart, He is going to guide you to do certain things for Him. He could even tell you to let go certain things you enjoy. These could be things that others do at ease. He could place you on a fast, he could give you a prayer program, He could even stop you from eating certain things. He has personally told me never to taste alcohol. I encourage you to obey Him promptly and fully. Not long ago the Lord told me that whenever He asks someone to consecrate it is a sign of deep love. Consecration is the key that opens the door to the supernatural life of God and the anointing. If you are not favored, He will never point out to you what you have to let go for the anointing to come in. Your life will move from glory to glory you decrease and allow Jesus Christ to increase in you.

PRAYER POINTS

1. *Lord, forgive and cleanse me from the self-life (selfishness, love of pleasure, greed, self-protection, fear to suffer for the Lord) and any sin in me that hinders me from sacrificing for the work of the kingdom.*

2. *Lord, deliver me from the grips of shallow Christianity.*

3. *O Lord, let your light shine in the Church again and cause us to understand the full meaning of your cross.*

4. *O God of all mercies, take hold of all your servants who preach to us so that they will take us to the cross for mighty spiritual breakthroughs.*

5. *Lord, restore the spirit of sacrifice in the Church, that we will please you.*

6. *Heavenly Father, open my spiritual eyes to see the sacrifice I must make for the release of your power in my life.*

7. *O Lord, give me the grace to pay any required price for the fulfillment of my destiny fulfillment of my destiny.*

8. *O Lord, show me any sacrifice you want me to make this year in order to experience a hundredfold harvest.*

9. *My Father, baptize me with unquenchable fire and zeal for Christian service.*

10. *O God of John the Baptist, touch the lips of all your children in this nation with fresh fire to preach the living gospel.*

11. *Let the fire of the Holy Spirit consume the curse of disobedience in my life.*

12. *Lord, inject me with supernatural grace for prompt and total obedience.*

13. *Let a fresh anointing of generosity for sacrificial giving pour on the church.*

14. *My Father, remove the heart of stone in me and give me a heart of flesh.*

15. *O Lord, make a difference in my life. Let those who do not know you see you through my life.*

16. *Lord, raise preachers in this land who will faithfully preach the message of the cross that saves and delivers.*

17. *O Lord, give us true men and women of God who will take us to our promise land.*

DAYS 8-9:
THE KEY OF SACRIFICE

Read: *John 12: 24-26, Romans 12:1-3*

Sacrifices will undoubtedly release supernatural power into your life. Throughout the history of the church, those who have understood this principle lived victories lives and left behind impeccable legacies when they died. You can begin to tap into this supernatural power as you begin to lay willingly and freely on God's altar any sacrifice, He demands from you.

What happens when a sacrifice is released?

1. There is multiplication through death
"Most assuredly, I say to you, unless a grain of wheat falls into the ground and dies, it remains alone; but if it dies, it produces much grain." (John 12:24).

Jesus Christ willing offered His life on the cross as a sacrificial lamb for the salvation of mankind. After that sacrifice He has been harvesting uncountable sons and daughter from all the tribes of the earth for more than 2000 years. He made more disciples after his death than before. The key to an abundant spiritual life is sacrifice. Sacrifice or the cross is the only weapon that can crush the power of the flesh in you and release you into the supernatural life of the Holy Spirit. Unfortunately many Christians protect their carnal nature and will not want it to face the cross.

Sacrifice is also the key to financial multiplication. **"He that goeth forth and weepeth, bearing precious seed, shall doubtless come again with rejoicing, bringing his sheaves with him."** **(Ps.126:6).**

If you refuse to release your seeds into the ground, you will never see multiplication. If you refuse to release your money for God's work or for investment, you will never see increase.

The church of God is stagnating spiritually, numerically and financially today because the spirit of sacrifice is absent among the believers. Have you realized that the more world leaders are trying to stamp out terrorist movements, the more they multiply? The cause of this unstoppable multiplication is the spirit of sacrifice. These terrorists do not love their lives above their mission. They are ready to die for their beliefs. We need the restoration of the spirit of sacrifice in the body of Christ. The gospel will spread to every corner of the world. Church projects will not suffer disgrace again. Christians will be so committed to the mission of the gospel that even threats of death will not cause them to compromise.

I have always been challenged by the testimony of the late Professor Zacharia Fomum the founder of the Christian Missionary Fellowship International who gave more than 90% of all his income for the work of missions. Do you know that as a result of this in less than a quarter of a century his organization was able to send and support missionary couples in more than 60 countries of the world?

Release your all to Jesus Christ and start to experience the power of multiplication in all the areas of your life. As a Christian if you have not yet learned to give God your tithe, when shall you begin to give Him your
Isaac?

2. Preservation of life
"He who loves his life will lose it, and he who hates his life in this world will keep it for eternal life." (John 12: 25).

We have eternal life today because Jesus Christ accepted to die for us. Do you see the power of sacrifice? The spiritual lesson we can learn from this is that the best way to preserve your life is to sacrifice it.

What does it mean to sacrifice your life for preservation? We will learn from Jesus' example.

"For He made Him who knew no sin to be sin for us, that we might become the righteousness of God in Him." (2Cor.5:21).

Jesus accepted to become a sinner eventhough He had not committed any sin because that was the only means by which we could be saved. He displeased Himself to please us. He gave up His life so that we can gain eternal life. He did this to teach us how we must live.

The Bible says,

"He died for all, that those who live should live no longer for themselves, but for Him who died for them and rose again." (2Cor.5:15).

Every sincere Christian knows that Christianity is about pleasing Jesus Christ and not self.

Today many innocent babies are being killed through abortion because people do not want to sacrifice. They only think about themselves and not about the destinies of those innocent children. Perpetrators of this evil act present selfish arguments like; "the baby would disturb their studies." Do you know that child bearing and nurturing is a great sacrifice? I want to appreciate all those who are laboring every day for the preservation of human lives. Medical researchers have had to risk their lives searching for solutions to human health problems. During the Japan nuclear disaster in 2011, I saw scientist risking their lives to quench reactors that were emitting massive radiation. Some of the scientific inventions we enjoy today costed the lives of some passionate researchers. Today we are enjoying the gospel in Africa but you must not forget that young American and Europeans sacrificed their lives for it. We have been told that in the 18th and 19th Centuries, Africa was called the "white man's grave." Many Europeans who came to Africa died from malaria. Some of the young people came in with their coffins prepared for any eventuality. Some of them actually died a few weeks after arrival and their corpses were transported back home.

The principle has not changed. If you are ready to die pleasing God, your life and that of others will be preserved. What is released to God will be preserved but what you keep that must be released will be taken away from you. Any money that must be given to God that you keep will be taken away by Satan. Your time that is supposed to be given to God that you keep shall be occupied by the devil.

3. Sacrifices Bring Honor

"If anyone serves Me, let him follow Me; and where I am, there My servant will be also. If anyone serves Me, him My Father will honor." (John 12:26).

Word serve is Gk *"diakoneo"* which means to be an attendant. It is costly to serve Jesus Christ because you must become a servant. A servant has no rights of his own. A servant has to follow the master even when he is not very willing and to places he may not like. Sometimes Jesus Christ the good Shepherd leads the sheep to the Promised Land through the wilderness.

The next challenge is that of satisfying the will of the master. If ever you have served any master you should have realized that it is not easy to meet up with the demands of a master. The good thing is that the Lord Jesus Christ empowers His servants with the anointing to do His will. He does not leave

the servant to struggle alone; He is always there to instruct and give assistance.
(Mat.28:20).

Above all He makes it very clear that those who pay the price and serve Him faithfully would be honored greatly.
If anyone serves Me, him My Father will honor."
(John 12:26).
"Those who are wise shall shine Like the brightness of the firmament, And those who turn many to righteousness Like the stars forever and ever." (Dan.12:3).

The unfortunate thing today is that many children of God want to be served and not serve. Some want they honor but do not want to sacrifice. They want the crown but not the cross. In church Christians prefer pulpit ministries and not secret ministries. Some Christians are perpetual spectators who are doing nothing to advance the work of the kingdom. I encourage you to identify your place in the body of Christ and begin to serve God sacrificially. Put in all you can to see things work for the glory of God. He will bless you and your family. No one can serve God faithfully and go empty handed.

Pastor Dag Heward Mills in his book *"Take Up Your Cross: A Call to Sacrifice"* also mentions four other powers that are released through sacrifice: The Power to make people follow; The power to make people believe; The power to induce commitment and the Power to make people take you seriously.

PRAYER POINTS

1. *Take time to thank, praise and worship God for who He is and for what He is doing in your life during this time.*
2. *Lord, deliver me from self and any sin in me that hinders me from sacrificing for the work of the kingdom.*
3. *Let every yoke of shallow Christianity upon y life scatter by fire.*
4. *Lord Jesus, teach me how to carry my cross daily and follow you.*
5. *O Lord, give me grace to pay the price for the manifestation of my destiny.*
6. *Lord, teach me to live for others too and not only for myself.*
7. *O Lord, restore the spirit of sacrifice among your children.*
8. *Lord, make me an unbreakable Christian.*
9. *O Lord God of Daniel, teach me how to fast for divine intervention.*

10. *My Father, restore the zeal for fasting and prayer in the church.*

11. *Lord, loose my heart and my hands and make me an aggressive giver.*

12. *Lord, Jesus make all your children committed soul winners.*

13. *Heavenly Father, release fire on the Church in this nation for a release of missionaries.*

14. *Let the fire of God fall on the church for the manifestation of aggressive prayer warriors.*

15. *Let the fire fall for the manifestation of Lion hearted evangelists who will set this nation ablaze for God.*

16. *O Lord, raise at least one Preachers of righteousness for every pulpit in every church in this land.*

17. *O Lord, raise Missionaries with fire who will go to the Islamic nations with the gospel.*

18. *Let the fire of God recruit of true servants in the church in this nation.*

19. *O Lord, release your anointing for the manifestation of committed people to lead miniseries in the churches.*

20. *O God of revival, flush out any form of entertainment from our pulpits.*

21. *O Lord of the church, flush out Esaus and Judases, from the leadership of our churches.*

22. *O God of Elijah, expose and cast out false prophets from our midst in Jesus' name.*
23. *Heavenly Father, release fresh rain and quench any strange fire that is burning in on the altars of our churches and families.*
24. *O Lord, release a fresh fire of purification on the churches for the restoration of holiness.*

DAYS 10-11:
IDENTIFYING STRONGHOLDS

Read: *2Corinthians 10:3-6*

The process of deliverance often consists of two main parts: Tearing down legal strongholds or removing rights and then casting out the demons. If you try to cast out demons without taking away the strongholds or legal rights that they are holding onto, then you can't really expect to achieve a complete successful deliverance. Removing these two blockages is vital in going about a complete and successful deliverance.

What Is a "Stronghold"?

"For the weapons of our warfare are not carnal, but mighty through God to the pulling down of strong holds" (2Cor.10:4).

This term has been greatly abused amongst many Christians who believe and practice spiritual warfare. If you ask different Christians what "strongholds" are, you would be shocked by the varying answers. It is therefore very important that we seek to understand what the Bible actually means when it uses the term "strongholds."

A stronghold is a demonic fortress. The word "strongholds" (Gr. *ochuroma*) occurs only once in the New Testament. According to some Bible scholars, it was used in New Testament times to denote "fortress" or "prison".

Satanic Deception

A stronghold is a faulty thinking pattern based on lies and deception of the devil. Deception is one of the primary weapons of the devil, because it is the building blocks for a stronghold. What strongholds can do is cause us to think in ways which block us from God's best. For example, if you think you have to confess all your sins to everybody you've ever wronged, you'll feel just awful and guilty until you do all that, and even then, you'll probably feel guilty, because you probably forgot many people that you didn't confess your sins to. All unnecessary, and a waste of time, all because you were deceived and thought that you had to do something that you really didn't have to do.

Demonic Legal Rights

Demonic legal rights are also called "footholds."
"In your anger do not sin": Do not let the sun go down while you are still angry, and do not give the devil a foothold." (Eph.4:26-27) NIV.

A legal right is something that gives demons an opportunity to enter or harass you, or gives them the right to remain in you even when we try to cast them out. Some of the most common legal rights that have given demons the power to dominate many people are:

Sins (especially willful sins)

When you commit sin, it gives the enemy a legal right to afflict or torment you in one way or another. The deeper the sin, the bigger the door that is opened to the devil. As long as the sin is there it is absolutely impossible to liberate that individual from satanic captivity. That sin becomes a stronghold that must be pulled down.

Soul ties

Soul ties are spiritual bridges or connections that bind two persons. Some of the most popular and destructive soul ties are formed during an adultery or fornication. 1 Corinthians 6:16 warns us not to

116

have sexual relations with a prostitute because we become one flesh (flesh as in soul realm kind of flesh, not a physical flesh) with that person. These soul ties serve as legal grounds through which the devil torments some people. (I will explain this in greater details later).

Demonic vows

Demonic vows are done with the devil when people join a cult, a witch coven, a gang, etc. Demonic vows can be made consciously or unconsciously. Such a vow is like a spiritual signature that the enemy uses as a legal right to gain access into someone's life. Often it is only when the individual renounces these vows that he/she can be delivered from the grips of evil spirits.

Unforgiveness

"But if you do not forgive men their trespasses, neither will your Father forgive your trespasses." (Mat.6:15).

When you refuse to forgive those who have offended you open your life to satanic attacks. Unforgiveness is one of the common footholds Satan is using to keep many people in captivity. Read Matthew 18:23-35, and keep in mind that the tormenters Jesus is referring to are demons.

Childhood abuse and rejection

Much demonic bondage is caused during childhood. For example, if a parent shows rejection toward their child, a spirit of rejection may enter. Some children have been demonized through rape and other forms of abuse. All these experiences create deep wounds in the hearts of the victims. If nothing is done about it, strongholds take root and these individuals become captives of the enemy.

Points of weakness

When the person experiences weakness, such as emotional shock, physical trauma, fearful experiences during childhood, and other areas to which the natural walls of defence in the physical, spiritual or emotional system of a person are weakened, it leaves you vulnerable for the enemy to attach himself to you. The devil always tries attack that weak area of your life. Someone who has been a drunkard or a drug addict in the past will likely face attacks in that area of his/her life.

Spoken self-curses

The words we say have spiritual value, the Bible says to bless and not curse, and that the tongue has the power of life and death (Prov.18:21). If you walk around saying, "I wish I could just die," a demon may hear you and can go to God and say,

"Look, she wants to die!" and here comes a spirit of death. Some people are actually struggling with self-imposed bondages.

"Death and life are in the power of the tongue: and they that love it shall eat the fruit thereof." (Prov.18:21). "You will have to live with the consequences of everything you say" GNT.

Cursed objects

Physical objects can carry spiritual value, such as idols, occult books, rings, movies, charms, etc. If you brought any accursed objects into your home, you could be opening the door for demons to enter and bother the people within your home. As long as these objects are there, the evil spirits cannot go. You have to burn them as commanded by the Lord (Deut.7:5, 25-26).

PRAYER POINTS

1. *Take time to thank and worship God for who He is and for what He has done in your life.*
2. *Thank God for the truth He has revealed to you through the teachings in this book.*
3. *In the mighty name of Jesus, I open my heart to truth of the word of God.*

4. *I submit all the areas of my life to the authority of God's word in Jesus' name.*

5. *O Lord, forgive and purge my spirit and soul of every wrong belief I have accommodated.*

6. *Lord, nullify the evil influence of family strongman upon my life in the name of Jesus.*

7. *Every stronghold of family strongman upon my spirit, soul and body, be shattered to pieces in the name of Jesus.*

8. *Let the wickedness of the family strongman be overturned in the mighty name of Jesus.*

9. *I arrest the spiritual soldiers of any family strongmen watching over the affairs of my life in the name of Jesus.*

10. *Let the thunder of God strike every altar of family strongmen in the name of Jesus.*

11. *I cancel the evil dedication of my name to any evil family strongman in the name of Jesus.*

12. *I bring the Blood of Jesus over every evil claim from the family strongman over my life in the name of Jesus.*

13. *I break the yoke of any family strongman upon my life in the name of Jesus.*

14. *Every foundation of family strongmen rooted in my dreams, visions and destiny, be uprooted in the name of Jesus.*

15. *I bind every strongman holding my privileges and rights captive, in the name of Jesus.*

16. *I retrieve all properties from the satanic banks, in Jesus' name.*

17. *I possess all my possessions, in the name of Jesus.*

18. *Lord, restore seven-fold, everything that spiritual thieves have stolen from me.*

19. *I bind every spirit sitting on my possession, in the name of Jesus.*

20. *I command my money being caged by the enemy to be completely released in the name of Jesus.*

21. *Let the riches of the Gentiles be transferred to me and the church, in Jesus' name.*

22. *I recover my blessings from water, forest and satanic banks, in the name of Jesus.*

23. *O Lord, create new and profitable opportunities for me.*

24. *Let the fire of the Holy Ghost burn the veils of religion that have blinded my family members and the people of this city from coming to Jesus Christ.*

25. *O Lord, release fresh fire for revival in the church in this nation.*

DAYS 12-13:
PULLING DOWN STRONGHOLDS

Read: *2Corinthians 10:3-6*

Once you have taken time to identify strongholds in your life, you have to follow the steps I will be presenting in this section for your breakthrough to come. Before we begin examining those steps, let me correct an error that the devil has been using to confuse some people. Often when people pray to pull down strongholds, you hear them attacking rivers, mountains, the grave yard etc. In their minds, they see demons gathered on a certain mountain top. The truth is that the strongholds you have to pull down are in your mind. Forget about all the demons in the seas, rivers, mountains and in your village. If you are free in your mind, even Satan himself will not do you anything. Jesus was not afraid of Satan and demons because He was not oppressed in the mind.

I will no longer talk much with you, for the ruler of this world is coming, and he has nothing in Me. (John 14:30).

Truth Confrontation

"For the weapons of our warfare are not carnal, but mighty through God to the pulling down of strong holds."

Strongholds are birthed and dwell in deception (which are lies and false beliefs), so naturally the cure is to bring the truth in God's Word on the scene. You demystify the lies of the enemy with the truth which is in the Word of God. The Bible says that our weapons are mighty for the tearing down of strongholds (2 Cor.10:4).

What is our primary offensive weapon? The sword of the Spirit, which is the Word of God (Eph.6:17). Truth dispels deception and lies, and therefore the more truth you bring into a situation, the more the darkness must flee. This is where it's important to grow in God's Word, is because it is your primary weapon for tearing down the strongholds of deception that the enemy has been feeding you. Jesus tells us that we can be held in bondage due to strongholds in our lives. And His solution was to, **"continue in my word... and ye shall know the truth, and the truth shall make you free." (v. 32-32)**

Get your Bible or any good Christian literature and read what God says concerning that particular stronghold you have identified. For example if it is sexual immorality do the following: Read Bible verses that condemn immorality, read verses that speak about our victory over sin through the work of Jesus Christ on the cross, also read verses that explain how one can be freed from the bondage of sin. All these scriptures will paralyze the strength of the stronghold on your mind.

Renounce the Wrong Belief
"But reject profane and old wives' fables, and exercise yourself toward godliness." (1Tim.4:7).

Satan controls people through wrong and profane beliefs. As soon as you identify such negative beliefs that do not agree with the truth of the Bible, openly renounce them. When you renounce them from your spirit, the devil loses his legal right over you. Open and firm renunciation is very powerful. It is a deadly blow to demonic manipulations. Many times during deliverance sessions I noticed that demons start manifesting and leaving when the victims begin to renounce wrong beliefs, evil covenants and sin.

One other thing I noticed is that some people fear to open their mouths and renounce the activities of the devil in their lives. Not long ago a woman came to me and requested that I should pray for her to be delivered from demonic oppressions. When I began questioning her I discovered that she was a "Nkamsi"; a soothsayer. She believed that the spirit of divination that was in her came from God. I took time to explain to her from the Bible that she was deceived but she was not really convinced. I finally told her that she had to renounce those spirits and all that she has been told by her family and other witch doctors before I pray for her. I was shocked that she postponed the prayer and till today she has never come back. This is what the Bible says,

"And have no fellowship with the unfruitful works of darkness, but rather expose them." (Eph.5:11).

Attack them With Scriptures

At this level you use the sword of the Spirit (the word of God) in two directions. First, you have to remind the devil and his demons that they have been defeated and therefore have no authority over you again. Remember that when Jesus faced the devil He kept declaring "it is written." Jesus actually used scriptures to give Satan a technical knockout. When you use scriptures to attack the demons behind the strongholds in your life, be very firm and aggressive.

"Be alert, be on watch! Your enemy, the Devil, roams around like a roaring lion, looking for someone to devour. Be firm in your faith and resist him," (1Pet.5:89) TEV.

Second, you have to face the strongholds in your spirit and soul with scriptures. There are three categories of scriptures you have to use in your battle against strongholds: scriptures that condemn that particular sin or situation, scriptures that speak about what God has done to free you from that particular sin or situation, scriptures that speak about the way of freedom from that sin or situation and scriptures that teach about the blessings of righteousness. There are also three ways you can use Bible verses to scatter strongholds in your life: you memorize the verses, you confess them regularly or you keep meditating on them. When you do this, the voice of the enemy is silenced. This strategy is very useful for people who are being harassed by evil thoughts.

Aggressive Prayer
"And from the days of John the Baptist until now the kingdom of heaven suffers violence, and the violent take it by force." (Mat.11:12).
"The effectual fervent prayer of a righteous man availeth much." (Jam.5:16b) KJV

The prayer that will demolish strongholds in your life must be very aggressive. James uses the statement *"effectual fervent"*. The statement is translated from Gk. *"energeo"* which also means to be active, be mighty in, work, hot. Prayers that produce mighty results are prayers that involve the whole man.

Make up your mind to pray until you experience change. Pray long and deep. I am often embarrassed by the way some people pray during deliverance or prayer meetings. They pray as if they had another place to go for help if God did not answer them. Some people even sleep and snore during prayer meetings. Some prayer meetings are as cold as a grave yard. I am convinced that one of the reasons why we have many unanswered prayers stems from the fact that people are nonchalant in their prayers. If all your hope is on God, you better pray with your whole life. No stronghold can resist you if you will position yourself in Christ and pray fervently.

PRAYER POINTS
1. *Take time to thank and worship God for who He is and for what He has done in your life.*
2. *Thank God for the truth He has revealed to you through the teachings in this book.*

3. *In the mighty name of Jesus, I open my heart to truth of the word of God.*

4. *I submit all the areas of my life to the authority of God's word in Jesus' name.*

5. *O Lord, forgive and purge my spirit and soul of every wrong belief I have accommodated.*

6. *O Lord, nullify the evil influence of family strongman upon my life in the name of Jesus.*

7. *Every stronghold of family strongman upon my spirit, soul and body, be shattered to pieces in the name of Jesus.*

8. *Let the wickedness of the family strongman be overturned in the mighty name of Jesus.*

9. *I arrest the spiritual soldiers of any family strongmen watching over the affairs of my life in the name of Jesus.*

10. *Let the thunder of God strike every altar of family strongmen in the name of Jesus.*

11. *I cancel the evil dedication of my name to any evil family strongman in the name of Jesus.*

12. *I bring the Blood of Jesus over every evil claim from the family strongman over my life in the name of Jesus.*

13. *I break the yoke of any family strongman upon my life in the name of Jesus.*

14. *Every foundation of family strongmen rooted in my dreams, visions and destiny, be uprooted in the name of Jesus.*

15. *I bind every strongman holding my privileges and rights captive, in the name of Jesus.*

16. *I retrieve all properties from the satanic banks, in Jesus' name.*

17. *I possess all my possessions, in the name of Jesus.*

18. *Lord, restore seven-fold, everything that spiritual thieves have stolen from me.*

19. *I bind every spirit sitting on my possession, in the name of Jesus.*

20. *I command my money being caged by the enemy to be completely released in the name of Jesus.*

21. *Let the riches of the Gentiles be transferred to me and the church, in Jesus' name.*

22. *I recover my blessings from water, forest and satanic banks, in the name of Jesus.*

23. *O Lord, create new and profitable opportunities for me.*

24. *Let the fire of the Holy Ghost burn the veils of religion that have blinded my family members and the people of this city from coming to Jesus Christ.*

25. *O Lord, release fresh fire for revival in the church in this nation.*

DAY 14:
BREAKING THE YOKE OF FEAR 1

Read: *Isaiah 41:10-16, 2Timothy 1:6-7, Genesis 12:2-5, 3John2*

One of the bondages that you must deal with in your life is fear. Until you put fear under your feet you cannot reach your divine destiny. Fear is an instrument the devil uses to manipulate people. Fear is never from God because the Bible says, *"For God has not given us a spirit of fear, but of power and of love and of a sound mind." (2Tim.1:7).* Take note that anytime fear comes on you it is not from God but from the devil and his agents. There is no Bible verse that exhorts you to be afraid of any situation no matter the name. Instead the Bible teaches that the forces of nature and the forces of darkness should fear and dread us. God ordered all the beast of the earth to fear and dread man (Gen.9:2). You are commanded not to fear the evil words of men (Isa.51:7). You also exhorted not fear those who threaten to kill you (Ps.27:1-3). Jesus taught His disciples not to fear anything in this world because He has overcome the world for them (John 16:33). Actually there are 365 "fear not's'" in the Bible. This means there is one for

130

every day of the year. What is that problem threatening your life right now? I hear the Holy Spirit say, "fear not. It is well!"

By the grace of God, we are going to identify and deal with the kinds of fear that are tormenting people every day. Some people have actually become slaves to one or more of these kinds of fear. Until you deal with fear, you cannot walk in victory. Fear keeps its victims in bondage.

1. The fear of death
"Inasmuch then as the children have partaken of flesh and blood, He Himself likewise shared in the same, that through death He might destroy him who had the power of death, that is, the devil, and release those who through fear of death were all their lifetime subject to bondage." (Heb.2:14-15).

The Bible points out here that the fear of death which is that feeling that keeps reminding you that, "you will die" is a satanic power used by the devil to keep you in bondage. If you ask some people why they think that they will die, they will not tell you anything tangible. The thing is that the devil has just taken hold of their minds. Some people refuse to travel because they fear to die. There use to be a woman in my village who said that a car is a dead trap. She lived for many years and died without boarding a vehicle because she feared to die. Do you know that the fear of death can stop you from fulfilling your destiny? The Bible teaches us that Jesus died on the cross to free you from every fear of death.

"that through death He might destroy him who had the power of death, that is, the devil, and release those who through fear of death were all their lifetime subject to bondage."(Heb.2:14-15).

Today I break that fear over you with the blood of Jesus. Even if that sickness you have is a sickness unto death, go home in peace not in fear.

This is what you must do if you want to be free from the fear of death. First, surrender your whole life to Jesus Christ if you have not yet done so. Secondly, reject the wrong message you have in your mind. Fear emanates from a seed which is a wrong picture or wrong message you have conceived. Thirdly, use the weapons of warfare (word of God, blood of Jesus, etc.) to do a warfare concerning your mind. This means you have to aggressively pull down the stronghold of fear. Finally, keep reminding the devil and yourself that your life is in God's hand and it is well with you (Isa.3:10).

2. The fear of Failure

Some people are dominated by the fear of failure. They have a feeling that what they start will not succeed. Some never even take a step to do anything because they are convinced in advance that they will fail. This is a demonic manipulation. If you are under such bondage, I command the yoke to break now in Jesus' mighty name. Say Amen! God has promised to help those who fear Him to succeed.

"Fear not, thou worm Jacob, and ye men of Israel; I will help thee, saith the LORD, and thy redeemer, the Holy One of Israel." (Isa.41:14).

He has promised to command blessings on everything you lay your hand upon if you keep His commandments.

"The LORD will command the blessing on you in your storehouses and in all to which you set your hand" (Deut.28:8).

Every good work you have started with Him will be accomplished (Philp.1:6). Failure is not His will for your life. Go ahead and do what He has told you to do. From today you will begin to experience the help of the God of Jacob in your life (Isa.41:14). The yoke of failure is broken in Jesus' name. Somebody said,

133

"Failures are successful people who gave up while successful people are failures who refused to give up."

3. The Fear of Sickness

This kind of fear keeps telling you that, "you will be sick" so you live in anxiety. It could be that you have identified that your family has a generational disease that has been slaying people prematurely so the devil comes to preach to you every day that you too will die. For some they just dread some diseases until anytime the name of that disease is mentioned around them they shiver with fear. Some very stringent hygiene rules some people keep is a manifestation of the deep fear of sickness and not just preventive measures. God says, "fear not, I will help you." (Isa.41:14).

If you are in the covenant, remember that Jesus is your physician (Ex.15:26, 23:23-26). Your body is His temple. He will keep you from sicknesses. Above all, Peter is not James. You can remember the case of James Acts 12 who was beheaded by Herod. The Bible says that when the people of Jerusalem showed excitement about the act, he went on and arrested Peter too. But do you know that when the church began to pray for his deliverance, an angel came to the prison and liberated him? So Peter did not die like James. Your case is different. Keep your body free from sin and from eating what you should not eat. Exercise always. Practice fasting. God will keep you from sicknesses. You will not die before time (see Ex.15:26, 23:25-26).

4. The fear of poverty

Many people are threatened by poverty. Some fear that they will remain poor while others who are wealthy and successful dread the thought of becoming poor. Do you know that the high rate of corruption and embezzlement in our society today is born from this type of fear? Why do people enter into satanic covenants? Why are some involved with terrible and unimaginable secret societies? It is because they fear to remain poor or lose their wealth.

A friend of mind told me how certain very flashy woman came to his office one day for prayers. She had a terrible incurable wound on her upper leg. No one could know that she had such a sore except she showed you. She told my friend that she could not sleep in the night because of the excruciating pains. When my friend asked her how she got it, she said that a friend took her to a meeting somewhere in the city of Yaoundé in Cameroon and she received a wound in exchange for much money. She took him to her car and showed him a boot filled with bank notes. She said, "that is the cause of my problem." The Bible says place *"The blessing of the LORD makes one rich, And He adds no sorrow with it." (Proverbs 10:22).* Ask for it! Wait for it! Receive it! Also believe God to preserve it for you.

5. The fear of singlehood

This is the fear that keeps harassing the unmarried. There is a voice that keeps asking, "are you sure you will marry?" This fear has caused some to abandon the faith. Some are still in church but have lost their connection with Jesus Christ because sin has invaded their lives. Do you know that the first person that waited patiently for a spouse was Adam? He was indeed alone for long. Why didn't he settle down with one of the animals? He realised that he needed a wife had to wait for God to give him one at the right time. I pray that God will help you to wait. May you not miss heaven because of marriage in Jesus' name. Let my God break every power that says you cannot marry and let this miracle be accelerated in your life in Jesus' name. Waiting is not wasting. It is said, "He who laughs last laughs best." God is bringing your own.

PRAYER POINTS

1. *Lord, I thank you for the power in the blood of Jesus made available for me.*

2. *O Lord, forgive me for accommodating thoughts of fear. Cleanse me with the blood of Jesus.*

3. *O Lord, release your fire on my soul let every chain of the fear of robbers and demons in me to melt by fire.*

4. *My father, today I bind and cast out of my life any spirit of the fear of demons and the fear of robbers ..... (mention the fears that are tormenting you) in the name of Jesus.*

5. *O Lord, let any power that has been threatening and terrorizing me with fear be terrorized from today.*

6. *O Lord, I command any seed of the fear of ..... (mention the names) in me to die now in the name of Jesus.*

7. *My father, let every satanic yoke of the fear of ..... (mention the names) over me, my family and brethren catch fire!*

8. *O Lord, cause your fire to establish an unbreakable wall around my life, family and church in Jesus' name.*

9. *Lay your hand on your head and declare 7 times, "I will enjoy all that God has blessed me with in Jesus' name." "I am hid under the mighty hand of the Lord, no evil will befall me. Peace, security and*

prosperity shall be my portion every day in Jesus' name."

10. O Lord, release your fire on my soul let every chain of the fear of poverty and singlehood in me to melt by fire.

11. My father, today I bind and cast out of my life any spirit of the fear of poverty and fear to remain single in Jesus' name.

12. O Lord, let any power that has been threatening and terrorizing me with poverty and singlehood be terrorized from today.

13. O Lord, I command any seed of the fear of poverty and singlehood in me to die now in Jesus' name.

14. My father, let every satanic yoke of poverty and celibacy over me, my family, catch fire!

15. O Lord, cause your win of favor to blow in my life. Let the unmarried be blessed with their spouses in Jesus' name.

16. Lay your hand on your head and declare 7 times, "I will prosper and enjoy the fruit of my labor in Jesus' name." "I will not miss my time for marriage. I will marry the right person for the glory of God in Jesus' name."

17. O Lord, I command any seed of the fear of death in me to die now in Jesus' name.

18. My father, let every satanic drag net of premature death cast over me, my family catch fire.

19. *O Lord, give me the heart of a lion and cause me to dominate over the works of the enemy.*

20. *Lay your hand on your head and declare 7 times, "I will live and not die in Jesus' name"*

21. *O Lord, release your fire on my soul let every chain of the fear of failure and sickness in me to melt by fire.*

22. *My father, today I bind and cast out of my life any spirit of the fear of failure and sickness in Jesus' name.*

23. *O Lord, let any power that has been threatening and terrorizing me with failure and sickness be terrorized from today.*

24. *O Lord, I command any seed of the fear of failure and sickness in me to die now in Jesus' name.*

DAY 15:
BREAKING THE YOKE OF FEAR 2

Read: *Isaiah 41:10-16, 2Timothy 1:6-7, Genesis 12:2-5, 3John2*

One thing I see in the Bible is that God never allows His loved ones to live under the yoke of fear. He always sends a "fear not" message to them. Today this same message has come to you. God is saying, "fear not, it shall be well with you!" We want to continue to expose the fears you MUST kill in your life before they kill you. I encourage you to take time and confront any type of fear God is exposing to you through this book.

6. The Fear of Robbers

Some people live in constant fear of robbers. There is a thought that keeps telling them that robbers will attack them. This type of thinking is inspired by Satan to keep you in bondage. I remember a lady who ran away from her room one night because she kept thinking that robbers will visit her. When she returned the next morning all her belongings were stolen away. She had many neighbors. Had it been that she was there she should have raised an alarm.

We even suspected that some of her neighbors took advantage of her absence and stole her things.

You must make up your mind to believe what God is saying concerning your protection or you allow Satan to rule your mind. This is God's promise concerning you, **"Because you have made the LORD, who is my refuge, Even the Most High, your dwelling place, No evil shall befall you, Nor shall any plague come near your dwelling; For He shall give His angels charge over you, To keep you in all your ways." (Psalm 91:9-11).** If you believe, say Amen!

God will protect you and all He has blessed you with. Do not accommodate any fear of robbers in your heart. Somebody is reading this book today who has lost some valuables to robbers, God will restore to you double before the end of this year in Jesus' name.

7. The Fear of Demons

Some people live under the fear of demons, occultists, witches and wizards. It is a satanic strategy to keep you in this type of bondage so that you will not enjoy the joy of salvation. This type of fear causes you to think continuously about demons and enemies instead of Jesus Christ. This is what Jesus says concerning your authority over demons, **"Behold, I give you the authority to trample on serpents and scorpions, and over all the power of the enemy, and nothing shall by any means hurt you." (Luke 10:19).**

As a believer, you have authority over ALL the powers of the devil. What is that power that is causing you to tremble? Exercise your authority over it in Jesus' name. Any authority that is not exercised has no effect. Remind the forces of darkness that Jesus Christ has defeated them on the cross and has given you power over them.

8. The Fear of Man
"The fear of man brings a snare, But whoever trusts in the LORD shall be safe." (Prov.25:29)

When you fear a human being more than God, you become a captive. The word "snare" in the verse above describes the cage that is used to imprison a bird. There are people even some believers who have been caged by this type of fear. It could be that you fear that the person would kill you or that he/she will cut off the financial and material support they have been giving you. It may be you fear that the person would dismiss you from your job. Whatsoever reason that causes you to fear any man or woman to an extent that you would disobey the word of God to please them is devilish. You are supposed to respect everybody but you must never disobey God to please any man. Arise and challenge the fear of man in your life.

9. Other Kinds of Fear

The list of the different kinds of fear is very long. Some people fear to give to family members or others because they think that those individuals will bewitch them. Based on the word of God in Mathew 5:44-46 and Romans 12:14, you should do good to your enemies. Do not be afraid, obey the leading of the Holy Spirit.

Some people fear to be alone, some individuals cannot sleep when the lights are turned off because of fear, some people even fear what they do not know. Jesus Christ was never afraid. He is called the Lion of the Tribe of Judah. If He lives in you, then you are powerful. You don't have to allow fear rule you.

Challenge it and don't try to justify it.

"You are of God, little children, and have overcome them, because He who is in you is greater than he who is in the world." (1Jn.4:4).

PRAYER POINTS

1. *Lord, I thank you for the power in the blood of Jesus made available for me.*

2. *O Lord, forgive me for accommodating thoughts of fear. Cleanse me with the blood of Jesus.*

3. *O Lord, release your fire on my soul let every chain of the fear of robbers and demons in me to melt by fire.*

4. *My father, today I bind and cast out of my life any spirit of the fear of demons and the fear of robbers ..... (mention the fears that are tormenting you) in the name of Jesus.*

5. *O Lord, let any power that has been threatening and terrorizing me with fear be terrorized from today.*

6. *O Lord, I command any seed of the fear of ..... (mention the names) in me to die now in the name of Jesus.*

7. *My father, let every satanic yoke of the fear of ..... (mention the names) over me, my family and brethren catch fire!*

8. *O Lord, cause your fire to establish an unbreakable wall around my life, family and church in Jesus' name.*

9. *Lay your hand on your head and declare 7 times, "I will enjoy all that God has blessed me with in Jesus' name." "I am hid under the mighty hand of*

144

the Lord, no evil will befall me. Peace, security and prosperity shall be my portion every day in Jesus' name."

10. *O Lord, release your fire on my soul let every chain of the fear of poverty and singlehood in me to melt by fire.*

11. *My father, today I bind and cast out of my life any spirit of the fear of poverty and fear to remain single in Jesus' name.*

12. *O Lord, let any power that has been threatening and terrorizing me with poverty and singlehood be terrorized from today.*

13. *O Lord, I command any seed of the fear of poverty and singlehood in me to die now in Jesus' name.*

14. *My father, let every satanic yoke of poverty and celibacy over me, my family, catch fire!*

15. *O Lord, cause your win of favor to blow in my life. Let the unmarried be blessed with their spouses in Jesus' name.*

16. *Lay your hand on your head and declare 7 times, "I will prosper and enjoy the fruit of my labor in Jesus' name." "I will not miss my time for marriage. I will marry the right person for the glory of God in Jesus' name."*

17. *O Lord, I command any seed of the fear of death in me to die now in Jesus' name.*

18. *My father, let every satanic drag net of premature death cast over me, my family catch fire.*

19. *O Lord, give me the heart of a lion and cause me to dominate over the works of the enemy.*

20. *Lay your hand on your head and declare 7 times, "I will live and not die in Jesus' name"*

21. *O Lord, release your fire on my soul let every chain of the fear of failure and sickness in me to melt by fire.*

22. *My father, today I bind and cast out of my life any spirit of the fear of failure and sickness in Jesus' name.*

23. *O Lord, let any power that has been threatening and terrorizing me with failure and sickness be terrorized from today.*

24. *O Lord, I command any seed of the fear of failure and sickness in me to die now in Jesus' name.*

25. *My father, let every satanic yoke of failure and sickness over me, my family catch fire.*

26. *O Lord, give me the heart of a lion and cause me to dominate over the works of the enemy.*

27. *Lay your hand on your head and declare 7 times, "I will succeed in all my projects and I will be healthy in Jesus' name"*

DAY 16:
IDENTIFYING NEGATIVE INHERITED PATTERNS

Read: *Galatians 3:13-18, 29, John 8:31-36, Romans 11:16-1*

Often some of the deepest problems we are facing are rooted in something we can't control.

This is what we call negative inherited patterns or dysfunctional family behavioral patterns. These patterns were established before us. Even though we can't change or control our past, we can control our future through the choices we make today. Each of us can choose life and good things instead of curses and death.

Family Influences Passed Down

Family traits are often passed down from parents to children, and this cycle has been repeated for thousands of years. Some of these traits may be positive and beneficial— like development skills, valuing hard work, godliness, generosity or education. However, negative and destructive behavior is also passed down within families – like stealing, laziness, immorality, pride, wickedness, ungodliness, greediness or hatred for education.

When God calls us and opens our minds to follow His way of life, we may not be fully aware of how our new relationship with Him will not only change us individually, but can also have a wonderful influence on our descendants, impacting future generations. Many people selfishly live only for today. They don't understand or appreciate how one member of a family can impact other members. The Scriptures often remind us that it's important to "think generationally".

Consider God's instruction in the Ten Commandments that,

"I, the Lord your God, am a jealous God, visiting the iniquity of the fathers upon the children to the third and fourth generations of those who hate Me, but showing mercy to thousands, to those who love Me and keep My commandments" (Exodus 20:5-6).

It's easy to believe from this scripture that God simply punishes those who disrespect Him and blesses those who love Him. But God is not a vengeful and angry Father who intentionally punishes great-grandchildren for the sins committed generations earlier by others.

A better way to understand this scripture is to realize that family dysfunctions and their consequences are passed down from parents to children and from generation to generation. Curses are the result of breaking God's law, and many sins are perpetuated in the next generation by the poor example of the previous generation.

Negative family cultures

Many scriptures confirm that negative family cultures can be very destructive. You and I are also a product of our own family's heritage going back for many, many years. Some of the weaknesses we have are a result of them being passed down directly to us by our parents' or grandparents' personal examples. In some cases a family sin may go so far back that no one now knows where it began.

Studies show that families tend to reproduce their own culture and dysfunctions for generations. For example, selfish parents produce selfish children. An alcoholic parent is likely to produce alcoholic children. Spousal abusers often produce children who grow up and abuse their spouses or are abused by their spouses. Parents with negative lifestyles and attitudes tend to produce offspring who are unproductive and discouraged. For instance research has demonstrated that approximately 90 percent of people imprisoned in the United States have had either a parent or close family member in jail before. Habitual problems may go back for generations in your family, but you can be the Abraham or David in your lineage. You can be the one to make better choices and break the curse of generational negative patterns in your family.

Abraham's example

A number of biblical passages show us why we should all think generationally. Perhaps the most striking is the example of Abraham. Abraham was an obedient "friend of God." He rejected the sinful pagan culture of his family line and chose to live a new and positive way of life. At God's request Abraham left that environment and even his own family to follow the course God set for him. In doing so he would become known as "the father of the faithful." (Gen.12:1-5). Because of Abraham's willingness to abandon the sinful habits and practices of his generation, God made specific promises to him about the future of his descendants. God told him,

"I will make your descendants as the dust of the earth; so that if a man could number the dust of

the earth, then your descendants also could be numbered" (Gnen.13:16).

Some of Abraham's descendants (Jews) formed the core of what are now known as the major English-speaking nations and many other nations. Almost 2,000 years later Jesus Christ, a direct descendant of Abraham was born – He atoned for all sins and offered eternal life to all mankind. The entire world came to be blessed through Abraham because of his willingness to break with the patterns of past generations and embark on a new way of life revealed by God.

David, a man after God's own heart

Another example of how powerful and important a personal relationship with God is can be seen in God's expression of love for King David.
"I have found David the son of Jesse, a man after My own heart, who will do all My will." (Acts 13:22).

From David's seed, according to the promise, God raised up for Israel a Savior—Jesus. (Acts 13:23) Jesus Christ was a descendant of King David, and both of them were physical descendants of Abraham. But did David's personal relationship with

God have any positive effect on any of his direct descendants, his great-grandchildren and beyond? Certainly, yes!

Abijah benefited from David's faithfulness

Abijah was the great-grandson of King David, who became a king 50 years after David but wasn't faithful to God's law. Scripture records that he did all the same sins his father before him had done. Abijah was not faithful to the Lord his God as David, his great-grandfather, had been. **"And he walked in all the sins of his father, which he had done before him; his heart was not loyal to the LORD his God, as was the heart of his father David." (1Kings 15:3).**

At first glance we might expect Abijah to be severely punished for his sins, and perhaps others along with him.

Yet the very next verse tells us something quite different:

"Because the Lord loved David, the Lord gave him a kingdom in Jerusalem and allowed him to have a son to be king after him. The Lord also kept Jerusalem safe" (1Kings 15:4) NCV.

152

You can see that more than 50 years after David died, God showed one of his descendants mercy because of the faithfulness of his great-grandfather. God said in effect, "I am not doing this for you, Abijah, but because of the relationship I had with your great-grandfather David, I will show mercy to you."

Hezekiah benefited from David's faithfulness

Many generations later King Hezekiah lay dying while the nation was being threatened by powerful Assyrian armies. The king fervently prayed to God for deliverance and the prophet Isaiah was sent to him with this message:

"Thus says the Lord, the God of David your father [ancestor]: 'I have heard your prayer, I have seen your tears; surely I will heal you. On the third day you shall go up to the house of the Lord. And I will add to your days fifteen years. I will deliver you and this city from the hand of the king of Assyria; and I will defend this city for My own sake, and for the sake of My servant David" (2 Kings 20:5-6).

More than 250 years after David died, God here showed mercy to his descendant because of David's personal relationship with God. Notice that God even identifies Himself as the "God of David" and proclaims that He will both heal Hezekiah and protect the nation for "the sake of My servant David." Again, God says in effect, "Hezekiah, I am not doing this just for your sake! I am doing it because of My relationship with your ancestor David." Do you see what a powerful influence just one individual can have, impacting his or her descendants for generations? Do you realize that you can be the Abraham or David in your family, setting a pattern that may bless your descendants from now?

After reading this section I believe that the Holy Spirit has helped you to identify some negative patterns that must be broken in your life and family. As you go on to pray, ask Him to help you identify any other thing that you have not yet discovered. If you are very desperate for a new beginning, I assure you that God's grace will be multiplied in your life for your breakthrough to manifest speedily.

PRAYER POINTS

1. *Thank God for divine revelation and for the grace of a new beginning that is coming on your life and family.*
2. *Worship God because He is able to change your situation and raise a new foundation for you and your family.*

3. *Thank and worship God for the price paid for your total deliverance on the cross.*

4. *Declare from your heart today, "My Father, I know that I know that from this day my life will never remain the same. A new man is emerging out of me in the name of Jesus."*

5. *Have you identified some sins and evil practices that you have been doing that are common with your family? Come to God now with repentance.*

6. *Ask God to forgive you for following the evil and sinful ways of your ancestors.*

7. *Forgive your ancestors for laying a wrong foundation for your family through these sins.*

8. *O God of Mercy, deliver me from .... (name the bondages. Example; immorality, pride, greed, stinginess, hatred, etc.) in the name of Jesus.*

9. *O God of mercy deliver my family from .... (name the bondages. Example; immorality, pride, greed, stinginess, hatred, etc.) in the name of Jesus.*

10. *My Father, take me to your divine theater room and deal with the root of the sin of...... (name it) in the name of Jesus.*

11. *My Father, let the sword of the Spirit put to death evil inherited character in my spirit and soul.*

12. *My Father, let your holy hand reshape me from inside to become like Jesus Christ.*

13. O Lord, let what must die in my life die! And let what must go, go! In the name of Jesus.

14. O God of Abraham, separate me spiritually from my earthly family line and connect me to the blessing of Abraham.

15. Let the fire of the Holy Ghost cut any spiritual umbilical cord that connects me to the evil of my family.

16. In the mighty name of Jesus, I command any yoke of collective captivity over my life to scatter by fire.

17. In the mighty name of Jesus, let the foundation of negative inherited patterns in my life catch fire.

18. In the mighty name of Jesus, let every bond of iniquity working in my spirit and soul die.

19. In the name of Jesus, let any other power opposing holiness and purity die today.

20. In the name of Jesus, let the stronghold of ungodly believes and practices in my life collapse today.

21. Dear Holy Spirit, give me no rest until I become what God wants me to be in Jesus Christ.

22. My Father, give me a new heart in the name of Jesus.

23. Lord Jesus, take your full place in my life from today.

24. I declare that I will not follow the evil ways of my ancestors.

25. I will fight and pull down any evil my ancestors introduced in my family. By the grace of God I will be a perfect example for the generations to come in the name of Jesus.

DAY 17: BREAKING NEGATIVE INHERITED PATTERNS

Read: *Galatians 3:13-18, 29, John 8:31-36, Romans 11:16-19*

Having understood what negative patterns are and how they affect families in the inherited previous section we want to go on to see how we can break out of them. Before we do that we shall examine the effects of inherited patterns in the lives of two families.

Two examples from history

How powerful can the generational influence of parents be on their own family and descendants? In 1874 a member of the New York State Prison Board noticed that six members of the same family were imprisoned at the same time. The prison board did some research, looking back a few generations to try to find the original couple who initiated this tragic family legacy. They traced the family line back to an ancestor – Max Jukes, born in 1720, a man considered lazy and godless with a reputation as the town troublemaker. Jukes had a drinking problem that kept him from holding a steady job. It also kept him from showing much concern for his wife and children. He would disappear sometimes for days and return drunk. He made little time for loving and instructing his children. To make matters worse, he married a woman who was much like himself, and together they had six daughters and two sons. Here is what the report revealed about the approximately 1,200 descendants of this couple who were alive by 1874:

- 310 were homeless.
- 160 were prostitutes.
- 180 suffered from drug or alcohol abuse.
- 150 were criminals who spent time in prison, including seven for murder.

The report also found that the State of New York had spent $1.5 million—a shockingly high number at the time—to care for this line of descendants, and not one had made a significant contribution to society. Sadly, we can see by this example how the harmful dysfunctions of parents can be passed down from generation to generation.

A refreshing contrast

In contrast, another family heritage was studied involving a couple who lived about the same time. This second family study began with the famous preacher Jonathan Edwards, who was born in 1703. A deeply religious man, he lived a life of strong moral values and became a minister and a dedicated family man. He married a deeply religious woman named Sarah who shared his values, and together they had 11 children. In no area was Edwards' resolve stronger than in his role as a father. Edwards and his wife Sarah had eleven children. Despite a rigorous work schedule that included rising as early as 4:30 a.m. in order to read and write in his library, extensive travels, and endless administrative meetings, he always made time for his children. Indeed, he committed to spending at least one hour a day with them. And what if he missed a day because he was traveling? He diligently made up the hour when he returned. Eventually, Jonathan Edwards became the president of Princeton University. Here is what researchers discovered about the approximately 1,400 descendants of Jonathan and Sarah Edwards by 1874:

- 13 were college presidents.
- 65 were college professors.
- 100 were attorneys.
- 32 were state judges.
- 85 were authors of classic books.
- 66 were physicians.
- 80 held political offices, including three state governors.

- 3 were state senators.
- 1 became vice president of the United States.

What a difference it makes in the kind of example and values that are passed down to the next generation. Strong moral values can indeed bring blessings and opportunities for generations yet to be born.

How to Break Negative Inherited Patterns

1. Identify them

You need to recognize what is happening and make a conscious decision to, with God's help, create a new, positive family legacy. The negative patterns will continue to pass on from one generation to the other until somebody identifies them and decides to put an end. As long as nothing is done, the cycles will continue to aggravate as we have seen above.

2. Repent

Repentance is the first step to break negative inherited patterns. You have to confess your sins and those committed by your ancestors as you are led by the Holy
Spirit.

161

3. Decide to bring change

The foundation of the every negative pattern is established on someone's wrong choice – sin against God. For change to come somebody along the line must choose to lay a righteous foundation. Choose not to continue in the wicked ways of your ancestors.

"I call heaven and earth as witnesses today against you, that I have set before you life and death, blessing and cursing; therefore choose life, that both you and your descendants may live." (Deut.30:19).

You are that person who will establish a new Abrahamic or Davidic foundation for your family. In want you to decide that if the history of your family shall be written 50 years from today, it should resemble that of Jonathan Edwards.

4. Put a stop to it

If you have a family legacy of negativity, addictions, poverty, divorce, greed or selfishness, put a stop to it. The good news is that we don't have to do this alone. God offers us the help of His Spirit so we can put a stop to these destructive habits and make life even more productive for our descendants.

5. Pay the price

It takes more than determination to change the future. It takes Christ. It takes His healing, unlearning negative patterns and then some relearning basic skills for life. Somebody must pay the price. This price could be prolonged prayers and fasting to deal with the sins of the family and spiritual warfare to demolish demonic strongholds. The price for a new foundation could also be adverse persecution from other family members who are not yet ready to change. If you can persevere on the way God is leading you, most of those opposing you will join you. Be ready to pay any price for a new foundation to emerge in your life and family.

6. Long and deep prayers

We are dealing here with patterns that have been established during many generations. It is not just rubbing some anointing oil on your head that will put everything back to order. You have to commit yourself to seasons of long and deep prayers together with consistent meditation on the word of

God until a new man in the likeness of Christ is formed in you.

"The earnest prayer of a righteous person has great power and produces wonderful results." (Jam. 5:16b).

Many have abandoned the faith in discouragement because they failed to settle down and work for new patterns to be established in their lives.

7. Build on the principles of God's word

The word of God alone has the power to reshape your whole life to become what God wants it to be. God has made the provision for your total restoration in the work Jesus Christ did on the cross. I encourage all those who want to break negative inherited patterns to be committed students of the word of God. Read, study, memorize and speak the word day and night in order to use it as a guide for all your choices and decisions. This will cause you to prosper in all your ways (Jos.1:8).

8. Ask for help

Some personal problems are so deep-rooted that we need to be humble enough to ask for help. Don't be hesitant to contact a minister or medical personnel if you continue to struggle with a problem and realize you need additional support. There is no shame in asking for help and encouragement from others.

9. Be a good example

A responsibility we all have is to root out these weaknesses and set a better example for our own children and grandchildren. This commitment to overcome our weaknesses and change our lives can also richly benefit our siblings, cousins, nieces, nephews, other extended family members and the whole society.

Having understood what negative inherited patterns are and how they affect families in the previous I want you to go into prayer believing that God will liberate you from every form of captivity and help you raise a new foundation for your life and family. Be determined that your story and that of your family shall be re-written.

PRAYER POINTS

1. *Thank God for divine revelation and for the grace of a new beginning that is coming on your life and family.*

2. *Worship God because He is able to change your situation and raise a new foundation for you and your family.*

3. *Thank God for exposing negative inherited patterns in your life and family.*

4. *Thank and worship God for the price paid for your total deliverance on the cross.*

5. *Thank God for the new page He has opened for you in this season.*

6. *Declare from your heart today, "My Father, I know that I know that from this day my life will never remain the same. A new man is emerging out of me in the name of Jesus."*

7. *Have you identified some sins and evil practices that you have been doing that are common with your family? Come to God now with repentance.*

8. *Ask God to forgive you for following the evil and sinful ways of your ancestors.*

9. *Forgive your ancestors for laying a wrong foundation for your family through these sins.*

10. *O God of Mercy, deliver me from …….. (name the bondages. Example; immorality, pride, greed, stinginess, hatred, etc.) in the name of Jesus.*

11. *O God of mercy deliver my family from …….. (name the bondages. Example; immorality, pride, greed, stinginess, hatred, etc.) in the name of Jesus.*

12. *My Father, take me to your divine theater room and deal with the root of the sin of...... (name it) in the name of Jesus.*

13. *My Father, let the sword of the Spirit put to death evil inherited character in my spirit and soul.*

14. *My Father, let your holy hand reshape me from inside to become like Jesus Christ.*

15. *O Lord, let what must die in my life die! And let what must go, go! In the name of Jesus.*

16. *O God of Abraham, separate me spiritually from my earthly family line and connect me to the blessing of Abraham.*

17. *O Lord, fill me with grace to live a life that is pleasing to you.*

18. *O Lord, give grace to build my life on your word.*

19. *In the name of Jesus, let any other power opposing holiness and purity die today.*

20. *In the name of Jesus, let the stronghold of ungodly believes and practices in my life collapse today.*

21. *Dear Holy Spirit, give me no rest until I become what God wants me to be in Jesus Christ.*

22. *My Father, give me a new heart in the name of Jesus.*

23. *Lord Jesus, take your full place in my life from today.*

24. *I declare that I will not follow the evil ways of my ancestors.*

25. *I will fight and pull down any evil my ancestors introduced in my family. By the grace of God I will be a perfect example for the generations to come in the name of Jesus.*

DAYS 18-19:
BREAKING CURSES 1

What is a Curse?

The word "curse" is often used in contrast with "bless" or "blessing." A curse is a declaration or prayer that calls for evil or harm on an individual. A curse is also a ban or censure over a person, place or thing. This curse, ban, or censure can be the result of a sinful act or disobedience to God's law. Often curses are spoken by servants of Satan.

A curse can also be defined as the absence of blessings. In the Bible a curse is the penalty for disobedience, as the blessing is the reward for obedience.

There are personal curses as well as generation curses. Personal curses are the retributions of one's personal sins while generational curses are passed down from parents to children. Let me point out here that the generational curse is not something directly passed down, but willingly accepted, for the scripture links the curse to a guilty party. The one who is under a generational curse is also guilty of some personal sins. Generational curses bring

169

judgment or bondage during an individual's life, reducing the quality of life, until that individual addresses the sin issues that put the curses into place. Moses addressed this issue when the Israelites were preparing to enter the Promised Land. He told the new generation that was preparing to enter in, that they would not enter unless they dealt with their own personal sins and also the sins of their fathers. The account can be found in (Leviticus 26:39-42).

But if they confess their iniquity and the iniquity of their fathers, with their unfaithfulness in which they were unfaithful to Me, and that they also have walked contrary to Me, and that I also have walked contrary to them and have brought them into the land of their enemies; if their uncircumcised hearts are humbled, and they accept their guilt- then I will remember My covenant with Jacob, and My covenant with Isaac and My covenant with Abraham I will remember; I will remember the land.

Whether the curse is personal or generational, the results are the same – untold hardship and pains. God is bringing this message to you at this time so that you can arise a deal with every curse that has been tormenting you. Jesus Christ has paid the price for your freedom so it is not proper that you continue to suffer!

How Do Curses Take Effect?

Curses take effect when you or your ancestors have committed certain acts which are contrary to the word of God. These acts of sin bring curses on you and your descendants. Demons try to perpetuate or re-enforce the curse for all remaining generations of the descendants. The demons can even enter the child in the womb at conception. This type of child comes into this world with certain strange characteristics. People may say that she was born like that but the truth is that the sins of her parents opened the door to demons to enter her life. Sometime ago, I prayed for a lady who was struggling with a serious incurable health problem. When I prayed and asked the Holy Spirit to open her eyes to see what was going on in the spirit realm, she told us that she was seeing eight demons dragging her with an umbilical cord. The Holy Spirit told me that the demons took hold of her right in the womb.

Re-enforcement of evil and pains
A curse ensures that the victim continues to sin so that divine judgment will be inevitable. We have

mentioned already that when sin is present demonic oppression is inevitable. Often for some people to be free or healed, sin must be dealt with after which the curse is broken.

An invisible hand the resists good

A curse is an invisible hand that fights and bars the way for good to come into your life. This explains the reason why a person who is under a curse labors harder than it is required to succeed.

A misleading force

A curse ensures that you make wrong choices in life. Do you know that your life is hanging on your choices? Those laboring under curses always miss the mark. The mark of divine blessing on one's life is the ability to make right and godly choices even in challenging situations.

Permit me say here that must always think thrice before you commit any act of sin. The consequences of your sins go beyond your life time. One act of adultery, bribery, fornication, false testimony or theft can derail your family line completely.

Origin of Curses

Where do curses come from? You must understand this without which you will go to the wrong place to look for solutions. I have seen Christians going to witchdoctors to wash them in order to remove curses. This is a product of ignorance. You can be baptized and confirmed in church but still be bound by ignorance if you refuse to study the scriptures. Take these statements of Jesus very seriously; **"Jesus said to the people who believed in him, 'You are truly my disciples if you remain faithful to my teachings. And you will know the truth, and the truth will set you free." (John 8:31-32)**

Curses come from God and are executed by Satan with permission from God. Curses can be found listed in the Bible. Satan cannot fabricate curses to place on you, he reenforces what the word of God has said already.
"But it shall come to pass, if you do not obey the voice of the LORD your God, to observe carefully all His commandments and His statutes which I command you today, that all these curses will come upon you and overtake you" (Deut.28:15).

With this understanding, you should go to God for deliverance whenever you identify a curse on your life or on your family. You should never allow anybody to lure you to witchdoctors. They are servants of Satan and he cannot remove what he didn't put.

How are Curses Identified?

1. We learn to recognize some curses by the names or characteristics mentioned in the Bible.
2. We can identify curses through experience. After dealing with many cases it becomes easy to identify others.
3. We can identify curses through the gifts of the Holy Spirit – the Holy Spirit impresses on your heart that an individual is under a curse.

Types of Curses

1. Psychic prayers

A psychic prayer is any prayer that does not line up with the word of God. If you pray contrary to the Bible then you are not praying to God but to Satan. Satan then has the right to released demons against the people you prayed against as well as yourself. Psychic prayer is a good way to curse others and be cursed n return.

2. Spoken curses

These are evil words declared against somebody. Thinking evil against somebody also falls in this line. Today some people are in pains because someone released a curse against them. Any curse spoken against you without cause will not stand but if you are guilty then you cannot escape until you make peace. **"Like a flitting sparrow, like a flying swallow, So a curse without cause shall not alight." (Prov.26:2)**

3. Ancestral curses

These are inherited curses that come on people because of sins committed by their ancestors.
"You shall have no other gods before Me. 'You shall not make for yourself a carved image-any likeness of anything that is in heaven above, or that is in the earth beneath, or that is in the water under the earth; you shall not bow down to them nor serve them. For I, the LORD your God, am a jealous God, visiting the iniquity of the fathers upon the children to the third and fourth generations of those who hate Me," (Deut.5:7-9).

We see here that children are under a curse because of the idolatry of their ancestors. But a child who

175

decides to follow the ways of the Lord and serve Him only will be free from such curses through the blood of Jesus shed on the cross (see Galatians 3:13-14).

4. Parental curses

The parents can curse their child. This can be in the womb, when the child is born and even when the child is an adult. Cursing a child in the womb includes: abortion attempts, conceiving the child in lust, not wanting the child when it is conceived. Examples of cursing the child after it is born include: rejecting the child in some manner such as wanting a boy when a girl is born, cursing the child in thoughts or words, mistreating the child mentally, physically, spiritually or materially such as physical, emotional and sexual abuse. When you abuse or neglect your parents curses also come on you.
"Cursed is the one who treats his father or his mother with contempt." (Deut.27:16).

You should never raise your voice or your hand against your parents no matter what they have done to you. The devil is just waiting for one occasion to pass on the curse that is already manipulating your parents to you, so run away when they provoke you.

176

Some children have actually abandoned their parents who labored to raise them in misery. You prosperity and peace will not last when you are living well and your parents are chaffing. Some children have abandoned their parents because they believe that they are witches or wizards. I think if they could not kill you when you were young and living with them, they will not kill you today that you are grown up and away from them. Above all you are a child of God. The Bible teaches us to do good to the wicked (read Matt.5:44, Rom.12:14, 20).

5. Cursing by others

You can be cursed by wicked people. The first group is Christians who pray psychic prayers against you. Such prayers will release demons against you. The second group includes: witches, wizards, occultists, fortunetellers and anyone practicing witchcraft or magic.

There must be a cause for such a curse to settle on you. If you are living an upright and blameless life, you should not be afraid – no curse will land on you no matter where it is coming from. Balaam tried many times to curse Israel but fail because there was no sin in her.

177

"But how can I curse those whom God has not cursed? How can I condemn those whom the Lord has not condemned? . . . God is not a man, so he does not lie. He is not human, so he does not change his mind. Has he ever spoken and failed to act? Has he ever promised and not carried it through? . . . No misfortune is in his plan for Jacob; no trouble is in store for Israel. For the Lord their God is with them; he has been proclaimed their king. . . . No curse can touch Jacob; no magic has any power against Israel. For now it will be said of Jacob, 'What wonders God has done for Israel!" (Num.23:8,19,21,23) NLT.

Any curse that is released against you without cause will unfailingly back-fire. Your part is to sustain a perfect relationship without God. Christians who live double standard lives will be victims in such cases. Do you know that after Balaam tried and failed he changed the method? He advised the Moabites to seduce the children of Israel to commit sin – idolatry and sexual immorality. When this happened, God Himself began to destroy them. Within a short time about 24.000 of them perished.

"But I have a few things against you, because you have there those who hold the doctrine of Balaam, who taught Balak to put a stumbling block before

the children of Israel, to eat things sacrificed to idols, and to commit sexual immorality." (Rev.2:14).

6. Self-imposed curses

Many people use their tongues to curse themselves. They say many negative things concerning their lives. Your tongue has power to build your life or destroy it. The Bible teaches that "life and death" flow from the tongue.
"Those who love to talk will suffer the consequences. Men have died for saying the wrong thing" (Prov.18:21) TLB.

If you want your life to take the proper shape, change the way you say concerning your very self.

7. Cursing your descendants

When you curse yourself, you also curse your descendants.

8. The curse of disobedience
"But it shall come to pass, if you do not obey the voice of the LORD your God, to observe carefully all His commandments and His statutes which I

command you today, that all these curses will come upon you and overtake you:" (Deut.28:15).

Those who disobey God's commandments open themselves to curses and demonic attacks. When things begin to go wrong with you ask yourself whether you are obeying God fully.

9. The curse of "charismatic witchcraft"

Witchcraft is the practice of trying to control others for personal gain. "Charismatic witchcraft" is exercising control over other Christians by leaders or anyone within the church for personal gain. This type of manipulation opens people up to demonic activities. Today we have many Christians who have been bewitched by some so called "men and women of

God." In some cases it is so serious that the lives of the victims are thrown completely out of balance – families are shattered, some have been duped, some abused and many other nasty things that should not be mentioned. No spiritual leader is called to control and manipulate Christians. Like shepherds, they are supposed to guide you and not dictate everything to you (Meditate on Psalm23). If Jesus Christ, the Lord of the church is not using force and manipulation to lead us, why should somebody try to bewitch you? You must never allow any individual to use their ministerial office to manipulate and control to do anything out of God's will. If you have become a victim of "charismatic witchcraft, breakout of it today in Jesus' name.

10. Cursed objects

Some people are laboring under curses because they have cursed objects in their possession.
"Neither shalt thou bring an abomination into thine house, lest thou be a cursed thing like it: but thou shalt utterly detest it, and thou shalt utterly abhor it; for it is a cursed thing." (Deut.7:26) KJV

If you have cursed objects on your body or in your possession that you carry around, or that bare in your home, then you are cursed by God. You have invited the demons to attack you and those living in your house.

Examples of cursed objects you can carry around include: charms, rings and talisman used for protection or luck; stolen clothes, shoes, watches, jewelry etc. that you are wearing; a stolen mobile phone; clothing carrying occultic symbols or things dedicated to demons; and stolen money.

Examples of cursed objects in your home include: idols; evil altars, magic books and materials like candles and incense; "anointed water" and "anointed oils" from evil sources; stolen things in your home; landed property gain fraudulently; etc.

You must carry out a thorough check of your house to identify what must be removed if the curse will leave you. Return what must be given back to the rightful owners, destroy with fire what must be burn and restitute what must be restituted. Even if the house you are living in or the car you are riding was gained fraudulently, return it to the rightful owners. Pay the price and receive the blessings of God that will last forever.

"And many who had believed came confessing and telling their deeds. Also, many of those who had practiced magic brought their books together and burned them in the sight of all. And they counted up the value of them, and it totaled fifty thousand pieces of silver." (Acts 19:18-19).

PRAYER POINTS
1. *Thank God for divine revelation and for the grace of a new beginning that is coming on your life and family.*

2. *Worship God because He is able to change your situation and give you what belongs to you.*

3. *Thank God for exposing curses in your life and family that must be dealt with.*

4. *Thank and worship God for the price paid for your total deliverance on the cross.*

5. *Thank God for the blessings He has made available for you in Christ Jesus.*

6. *If you have identified any curse in your life, ask God to forgive you for sinning against Him.*

7. *If you cannot trace the sin that opened the door to the curse, still ask God to forgive you for what you do not know.*

8. *Heavenly Father, I come in the name of Jesus to forgive my ancestors and anyone else that has cursed me.*

9. *In the mighty name of Jesus, I break any curses ….. (name them) that came on me and my descendants because of my own sins.*

10. *In the mighty name of Jesus, I break any curses …… (name them) that came on me and my descendants because of the sins of my ancestors.*

11. *In the mighty name of Jesus, I break any curse on me and my descendants that came through evil utterances and wishes made by whosoever.*

12. *I use the blood of Jesus to cancel every legal ground that demons have to re-enforce curses in my life in the name of Jesus.*

13. *In the mighty Name of Jesus Christ, I now rebuke, break, loose myself and my children from any and all evil curses, charms, vexes, hexes, spells, jinxes, psychic powers, bewitchment, witchcraft and sorcery, that have been put upon me or my family line from any persons or from any occult or psychic sources.*

14. *In the mighty name of Jesus, I bind all evil spirits connected to these curses and I command them to leave me now.*

15. *Father, in Jesus name, I take the authority You have given me in your word to trample over all of the power of my enemies, and to cast out any demons and unclean spirits that are trying to harass my life.*

16. *Father, in the name of Jesus, by operating under your full power and full authority, I now take authority over any curse line and break every single part of it that demons may be operating on.*

17. *In the mighty name of Jesus, I command every curse to be fully broken right now, now and forevermore!*

18. *Father, I believe that every curse line between my father, Mother and me have now been fully broken and the re-enforcing demons will no longer have any more legal right to continue to attack me.*

19. *Pray divine blessings upon your life and family. Ask God to fill your with good things. Use the prophetic prayers in chapter 6.*

DAY 20:
BREAKING CURSES 2

W e want to continue to examine the different sources of curses so that you can take time to find out whether there is an area of your life that you have to put in order. We have seen already that curses could be personal or generational. Whether the curse is personal or generational, the results are the same – untold hardship and pains. God is bringing this message to you at this time so that you can arise a deal with every curse that has been tormenting you. Jesus Christ has paid the price for your freedom so it is not proper that you continue to suffer!

General Sources of Curses

1. Those who curse and mistreat Jews (Deut.27:26, Gen.27:29).
2. Those who willingly deceive others (Jos.9:23, Mal.1:14).
3. An adulterous woman (Num.5:27).
4. Disobedience to God's commandments (Deut.28:15, Jer.11:3).
5. Idol worship (Jer.44:8, Ex.20:5).

185

6. Those who keep or own cursed objects (Deut.7:25,
   Jos.6:8).
7. Those who refuse to come to the Lord for help (Jug.5:23).
8. The house of the wicked (Prov.3:33).
9. He who gives not to the poor (Prov.28:27).
10. The earth by reason of man's disobedience (Isa.24:3-6).
11. Jerusalem is a curse to all the nations if Jews rebel against God (jEr. 26:6).
12. Thieves and those who sear falsely by the Lord's name (Zec.5:4).
13. Ministers who fail to give the glory to God (Mal,2:2, Rev.1:6).
14. Those who rob God of tithes and offerings (Mal.3:9, Hag.1:6-9).
15. Those who dishonor their parents (Deut.27:16).
16. Those who listen to their wives rather than God (Gen.3:17).
17. Those who make graven images (Deut.27:15, Exo.20:4).
18. Those who willfully cheat people out of their property (Deut.27:17).
19. Those who take advantage of the blind (Deut.27:18).
20. Those oppressing strangers, widows and the fatherless (Ex.22:22-24).

21. He who lies with his father's wife (Deut.27:20, Lev.18:8).
22. He who lies with his sister or brother (Deut.27:22).
23. Those who strike their neighbors secretly (Deut.27:24).
24. Those who take money to slay the innocent (Deut. 27:24).
25. He who lies with any beast (Deut. 27:21, Ex.22:19).
26. Adulterers (Job 24:15-18).
27. The proud (Psalm 119:21).
28. Those who trust in man and not the Lord (Jer.48:10).
29. Those who do the work of the Lord deceitfully (Jer.48:10).
30. He who keeps his sword from blood (1Kgs.20:35-42).
31. Those who reward evil for good (Prov.17:13).
32. Illegitimate children (Deut.23:2).
33. Children born through incest (Gen.19:36-38).
34. Murderers (Ex.21:12).
35. To murder indirectly (Ex.21:14).
36. Children who strike their parents (Ex.21:15).
37. Kidnappers (Ex.21:16, Deut.24:7).
38. Those who curse their parents (Ex.21:17).
39. Those who kill the unborn (21:22-23).

40. Those involved in witchcraft (Ex.22:18).
41. Those who sacrifice to false gods (Ex.22:20).
42. Those who attempt to turn anyone from the Lord (Deut.13:6-9).
43. Those who follow horoscopes (Deut.17:2-5).
44. Those who rebel against pastors (Deut.17:12).
45. False prophets (Deut.18:19-22).
46. Women who keep not their virginity until they are married (Deut.22:13-21).
47. Parents who do not discipline their children, but honor them above God (1Sam.2:17,27-36).
48. Those who curse their rulers (1Kgs.2:8-9).
49. Those who sacrifice human beings (Lev.20:2).
50. Homosexual and lesbian relationships (Lev.20:13).
51. Those who participate in fortune-telling (Lev.20:6).
52. Those who blaspheme the Lord's name (Lev.24:15-16).

Steps to Freedom from Curses

God's provision
The price for freedom from curses has been paid!

Your curse is transferred on Jesus
The Bible teaches that Christ was made a curse, so that we can be freed from the curses that sin (both

our sins and those of our forefathers) has brought us.

"Christ has redeemed us from the curse of the law, having become a curse for us (for it is written, "Cursed is everyone who hangs on a tree" (Gal.3:13).

The curse is stopped

The good news is that once you accept Jesus Christ as your personal Lord and Savior, the transference of bondages and curses stops.

"In those days they shall say no more: 'The fathers have eaten sour grapes, And the children's teeth are set on edge.' 'But everyone shall die for his own iniquity; every man who eats the sour grapes, his teeth shall be set on edge." (Jer.31:29-30).

Don't be ignorant!

Jesus Christ has paid the debt you owed and heaven has declared your freedom already. So why are there some believers who are still living under bondages? This is a major debate in Christendom. Many believe that a believer cannot be demonized. It is true, but what I have come to understand is that until you apply the victory of the cross on all the areas of the cross, the devil can still manipulate you. Some people came into the covenant (salvation in Christ) already demonized. Such individuals can continue to suffer under demonic oppressions for many years until these demons are cast out. So you should not be surprised that during ministration some believers start manifesting strangely. Cast out the demons and set them free. Don't try to argue the genuineness of their faith. They could have been genuinely born again but certain areas of their lives had been under demonic domination. Remember that only God has the power to remove your sins but he has given the authority to men to cast out demons. So sometimes after God has removed the sins, he expects us to cast out the demons.

Your part

1. Identify the name of the curse
Ask the Holy Spirit to help you identify the curse and the sin that brought it. Until you do this, you cannot break it.

2. Repent
Pray and ask God to forgive you for the sin. Also ask Him to take away the right for the curse to be in your life. Turning away from your sins is the first step for your deliverance from curses. If you cannot abandon sin then forget about divine blessings. There is no man of God that can force God to bless you when you continue in sin. Even protracted fasting cannot

force God to bless one who has refused to abandon sin.

3. Forgive your ancestors

Forgive them for opening the door for the curses to enter your family line.

4. Break the curse

Break the curse in the name of Jesus. Insist and be very firm.

5. Cast out the demons

Usually demons come in with the curse. Take authority over them and cast them out. This is the spiritual warfare dimension of breaking curses.

6. Discipline your life

Commit yourself to live according to the word of God. This is very important if the curse would go. The curse came in because of a bad life. You cannot be completely free from it until you abandon that bad way of life. Some people fast and pray for breakthrough after which the return to their old life. It cannot work like that.

7. Restitute

Sometimes in order to break the power of the curse completely, you have to carry out restitution.

Restitution simply means to pay back what you owed what you owed somebody or repair what you spoiled. For instance if you have sent away a worker without paying his/her wages, you are under a curse. If you want God to bless you, call the person and pay the money. If the individual has died, hand it to his/her family members.

8. Confess what is rightfully yours

Use the power of the tongue to establish your freedom. We know that our curses have been broken in Jesus' name, but learn to verbally confess what is rightfully yours, because there's power in our verbal confessions. Verbal confession helps us to realize that we are set free, and also lets the enemy know that he's in trouble.

Here's a great sample confession prayer you can use:

In the name of Jesus, I confess the sins and iniquities of my parents (name specific sins if known), grandparents (name specific sins if known), and all other ancestors. I declare that by the blood of Jesus, these sins have been forgiven and Satan and his demons can no longer use these sins as legal grounds in my life!

In the name of Jesus, and by the power of His blood, I now declare that all personal and generational curses have been renounced, broken and severed, and that I am no longer under their bondage!

In the name of Jesus, I declare myself and my future generations loosed from any bondage passed down to me from my ancestors.

It is well with me and my descendants. AMEN!

PRAYER POINTS

1. *Thank God for divine revelation and for the grace of a new beginning that is coming on your life and family.*
2. *Worship God because He is able to change your situation and give you what belongs to you.*
3. *Thank God for exposing curses in your life and family that must be dealt with.*
   Lay your hand on your chest and pray the following prayers from your heart. (if you are not yet born again, it is a waste of time trying to break curses. It is good you stop and surrender your life to Jesus first.)
4. *Dear Heavenly Father, I come to You as Your child, born again, redeemed, and washed in the blood of Jesus. I declare that You, Jesus, have redeemed me from the curse of the law having been made a curse for me at Calvary.*

5. *I proclaim that I am a partaker of the inheritance of the saints of God.*

6. *I give thanks unto You, Father, for delivering me from all the powers of darkness and translating me into the kingdom of your dear Son.*

7. *As one who is covered with the blood of Jesus, I here and now reject and disown all the sins, pacts, dedications, curses and occult activities of my ancestors or any relatives, specifically (name of person(s) responsible for the curse, if known), which has been passed on to me intentionally or unintentionally."*

8. *In Jesus' name, Father, I ask to be redeemed and cleansed from all evil curses, incantations, dedications, spells, pacts, and familiar spirits passed on to me from my parents, grandparents, greatgrandparents, ancestors, relatives, or any other person, specifically (name of person(s) responsible, if known).*

9. *My Father, I also ask to be redeemed and cleansed from all curses that have come upon me from what I have done or been involved in.*

10. *I now appropriate in my life, Jesus' death on the cross to free me from all curses. I REPENT and declare that I am totally committed and complete in my relationship to my Lord, Jesus Christ."*

11. *In the Name of the Lord, Jesus Christ, I now rebuke, break and loose myself and all my*

children or children to be, from all evil curses, charms, vexes, hexes, spells, incantations, jinxes, psychic powers, bewitchments, pacts, dedications, or sorcery that have been put on me or my family line or by any other person or persons (person's name, if known) or from any occult, cultic, satanic or psychic source.

12. *I declare all these curses, dedications, or pacts null and void, in Jesus' name.*

13. *In the mighty name of Jesus, I reject every way in which Satan may claim ownership of me. I reject every demon, evil spirit or familiar spirit sent to me by Satan or attached to any part of me because of these curses, dedications, pacts or my activities.*

14. *I command all the connected and related spirits to leave me now and never return, in Jesus' name.*

15. *In the mighty name of Jesus, I command you, Satan, to remove from me all satanic shields, seals, devises or mechanisms used to harass, manipulate, or control me in any way or attach and hold a familiar or demonic spirit to any part of me.*

16. *In the mighty name of Jesus, I command you, Satan, to take them off now, and I command all these attached spirits to leave me now and never return.*

17. *My Father, in Jesus' name, I ask you to send your warrior angels to take all these evil and familiar spirits to their destination.*
18. *Pray divine blessings upon your life and family. Ask God to fill your with good things. Use the prophetic prayers in chapter 6.*

DAY 21:
FREEDOM FROM SOUL TIES

Read: *1Corinthians 6:12-20*

What is a "Soul Tie"?

L et's start by considering the definition of a soul tie: A soul tie is the joining or knitting together of the bonds of a relationship. Godly soul ties occur when like-minded believers are together in the Lord: friends, marriage partners, believers to pastors, etc. Relationships that lack 'God-centeredness' can result in ungodly soul ties between friends, parents and children, siblings, marriage partners, former romantic or sexual partners, domineering authorities, etc. An unhealthy attachment with another can bring about a psychic (spiritual) control that can adversely affect the life, e.g. a mother who refuses to give up her hold on her children, a person who refuses to release to the Lord the memory of an old romantic relationships, a person who holds a grudge or a judgment against another, someone who uses spiritual forces to control others (witchcraft), etc.

The cause of spiritual problems

Negative or unhealthy soul ties constitute the root of some of the spiritual problems some people are suffering from. As long as the bond between you and the other party remains you are not free spiritually. Why is it that even after some people are married, they still sustain extra-marital affairs with their ex-sex partners? The answer is soul ties.

The old bonds have not been broken.

Formation of soul ties

For two people to bond to the point of a soul tie often takes time, particularly in the area of friendships. Man's soul consists of his mind, emotions, and will. A soul tie involves the joining of minds, ideas and views, as well as emotional unions in the feeling realm.

Four levels of soul ties

1. *The thread soul tie:* A 'thread' relationship would simply be an acquaintance; someone you greet at your job every day.
2. *The string soul tie:* A 'string' relationship would perhaps be an associate who you're more intellectually tied to, someone with whom you have certain things in common.

3. *The rope soul tie:* A 'rope' relationship would be a good friend, a companion and confidant, one in whom you would be free to 'be yourself' and share things about your life that are somewhat vulnerable.

4. *The cable soul tie:* Finally, a 'cable' relationship would be someone to whom you're related: your wife, your kids, and your immediate family.

Now, breaking a piece of thread is not difficult. In the same way, losing a casual acquaintance is not a big deal emotionally. Breaking a string may take some effort, and so the loss of an associate would affect you to some degree, depending on the depth and length of the relationship. A rope or a cable, however, would require tremendous effort to break, particularly if there was tension in the line. So it is that the loss of an intimate friend or family member can affect your soul tremendously. Healthy soul ties stabilize the soul while unhealthy soul ties generate all types of emotional traumas. That is why you should be careful not to hook up with the wrong people.

Types of Soul Ties

1. Marriage soul ties

The first mention of a "soul tie" in the Word is found in Genesis:

"So the Lord God caused the man to fall into a deep sleep; and while he was sleeping, he took one of the man's ribs and closed up the place with flesh. Then the Lord God made a woman from the rib he had taken out of the man, and he brought her to the man. The man said, "This is now bone of my bones and flesh of my flesh; because she was taken out of man, she shall be called 'woman'. For this reason a man will leave his father and mother and cleave unto his wife, and they will become one flesh." (Genesis 2:21- 24)

This is the famous "leave and cleave" passage concerning marriage. From the very beginning God's intention has been that the man and woman's soul ties with their parents should be broken prior to marriage. Why is that? Because when one partner is still emotionally tied to his/her parents, often there is unhealthy manipulation and control that destroys the marriage. So, interestingly enough, we see that the first

Bible reference to a soul tie is a caution to break a soul

tie. You must first break the soul tie with your family – especially your parents before you can be able to cleave to your spouse. Many marriages are in chaos today because the couples are unconsciously under the control of their parents. As long as this continues, it is impossible for real bonding to take place in marriage. God's order is that the relationship between husband and wife should be stronger than that of parents and children. When this order is reversed the marriage bond

breaks.

2. Friendship soul ties

We can see this type of soul tie between Naomi, Ruth and Orpah.

"...Then Orpah kissed her mother-in-law good-by, but Ruth clung to her. "Look," said Naomi, "your sister-in-law is going back to her people and her gods. Go back with her." But Ruth replied, "Don't urge me to leave you or to turn back from you. Where you go I will go, and where you stay I will stay. Your people will be my people and your God my God. Where you die I will die, and there I will be buried. May the Lord deal with me, severely if

need be, if anything but death separates you and me." (Ruth 1:14-17)

Ruth was bonded to Naomi like glue. In fact, the Hebrew word for 'clung' (dabaq) is a word similar to the one used in Israel today for 'glue'. So, we see they were "glued together" in a loving and faithful relationship of mother and daughter-in-law. Let's consider another example of a friendship-type soul tie: **"..when he had made an end of speaking to Saul, the soul of Jonathan was knit with the soul of David, and Jonathan loved him as his own soul." (1 Samuel 18:1)**

Jonathan, the son of King Saul, had great respect and love for David, the future king. The friendship was so deep that we're told their very souls were 'knit' together. This bonding served them both well in the days to come. Jonathan did his best to protect David from Saul's rage and David, when he became king, went to great lengths to care for Jonathan's only remaining son.

If you become knit like this with the wrong person, your destiny will be destroyed.

3. Soul ties with other believers
"I beseech you, by the name of our Lord Jesus Christ, that you all speak the same thing, that there be no divisions among you; but that you be perfectly joined together in the same mind and in the same judgment." (1 Cor. 1:10)
"I would that you knew what great conflict I have for you....that your hearts might be comforted, being knit together in love, and unto all riches of the full assurance of understanding, to the acknowledgment of the mystery of God the Father and of Christ;" (Col. 2:1-2)
In these verses, believers are encouraged to *knit* their lives together like threads in a garment, each thread intricately woven with each other. This is a picture of how God wants the body of Christ to be. However, soul ties among believers should really be called spirit ties. Believers are 'spirit tied' before they're 'soul tied'. When you experience spiritual rebirth, you become one in Spirit with every other believer. As a result, bonding in the mind and emotions becomes far easier, because of the spirit union already there.

This is the reason believers can meet somebody they've never met before and feel like they've known them for many years. Believers "bear witness in their spirit" when they meet someone who loves

Jesus. Satan cannot fake real joy or peace. And he particularly cannot counterfeit the love of God that flows spirit to spirit between true believers. You must ask God to bring you to this level so that you can really enjoy the Christian life.

4. Soul ties with pastors or spiritual leaders
"So every man of Israel left David, and followed Sheba the son of Bichri: but the men of Judah clave unto their king, from Jordan even to Jerusalem." (2 Sam. 20:2)

Here we see the men of Judah bonding with their leader David. This shows the soul tie that's needed between believers and their spiritual authorities. Again, the Hebrew word here is 'dabaq' for 'glue'. The men were *glued* to their authority – King David. We see a similar tie of devotion between Elijah and Elisha, Moses and Joshua, and Jesus and His disciples. Such a bond is needed for a pastor or spiritual leader to pass on anointed ministry to those submitted to him in the Lord. Those who are opened to the pastor catch his anointing. I tell members of my church that if anyone does not believe in the ministry God has invested in my life, he/she should locate another pastor. I say so because I know that you can never be blessed by a pastor you do not believe and submit to.

5. Soul ties between parents and children
"When I come to my father, and the lad is not with us, seeing that his life is bound up in the lad's life, then he will go down to his grave with sorrow and die.." (Gen. 44:30-31)

In this verse, we see a picture of a father so tied with his son that, were his son to fail to appear, he would go down to his grave with sorrow. Few ties are as tight as those between parents and their children, particularly between a mother and her child. God ordained such natural bondings, knowing that child rearing is difficult. At times, were it not for such soul ties, many parents might be tempted to give up. But with such ties, a parent can sustain a level of unconditional love essential for the proper development of the child.

5. Ungodly soul ties
A soul tie is a 'channel'. Think of a soul tie as a water pipe through which flows mental and emotional things. Spiritual things can pass through as well, be they from the human spirit, be they psychically induced, demonically inspired, or genuine and edifying from the Lord. Because demonic spirits can transfer so easily through soul ties, it's crucial to identify and destroy those that are ungodly,

controlling, or emotionally binding. Let's look at some examples of unhealthy soul ties:

a. **Ungodly soul ties between father and son God said, "Why do you kick at my sacrifice and my offering and honor your sons above me...? For I will judge his house forever..... because his sons made themselves vile, and he did not restrain them." (1 Samuel 2:29, 3:13)**

    God was rebuking the prophet Eli because of his unwillingness to correct his sons for their sins against the Lord. The sin of Eli was parental permissiveness. As a result, God's judgment came upon his house. Parents can develop soul ties of indifference, permissiveness, idolatry, compromise and control (and in many other areas). The results are often detrimental. What type of soul ties exist between you and your children or you and your parents? Deal with the wrong ones.

b. **Soul ties in unhealthy relationships "Make no friendship with an angry man; and with a furious man do not go: otherwise you'll learn his ways and get a snare to your soul." (Prov. 22:24-25)**

"Be not unequally yoked together with unbelievers: for what fellowship has righteousness with unrighteousness? What communion has light with darkness? What concord has Christ with Baal?...Come out from among them, be separate, and touch not the unclean thing; and I will receive you and will be a Father to you, and you shall be my sons and daughters, says the Lord Almighty." (2 Cor. 6:14-18)

We are clearly admonished in scripture to be wise in our relationships. We're told to avoid close associations with those that are angry, with those acting foolishly and with those that are unbelievers. Understand that we're not prohibited here from having *any* relationship with such persons. Rather, it's just that such relationships should not be able to form unhealthy soul ties where one's witness and walk with the Lord is compromised. Who are your closest friends? God is not a fool – He warns you to separate from ungodly friends for the sake of your soul.

c. **Soul ties through impure sexual activity**
"Dinah the daughter of Leah went out to see the daughters of the land. When Shechem saw

her, he took her, lay with her and defiled her. And his soul clave to Dinah, and he loved the damsel, and spoke kindly to her." (Gen 34:1-3)

"King Solomon loved many strange women.... concerning which the Lord said, you shall not go in to them, neither shall they come in to you: for they will turn away your heart after their gods: Solomon clave to these in love." (2 Kings. 11:1-2)

"Don't you know that your bodies are the members of Christ? Shall I then take the members of Christ, and make them the members of an harlot? God forbid. What? Don't you know that he which is joined to an harlot is one body? For two, says He, shall be one flesh." (1 Cor 6:15-16)

God's plan for a man and a woman is not at all like that of the world. First, He would have them come together and bond in the area of the spirit. Over time, as they get to know one another, a bonding of the mind and emotions would occur. Then, only after solemn vows of commitment in marriage, would any bonding of the body through sexual intercourse permitted.

The world has it backwards. Generally, people indulge in sexual activities with people they are not married to. Though a few of these relationships end up in marriage many fall out. The parties separate with wounded emotions. Some leave demonized and contaminated with curses.

The sexual route is the major highway for the transmission of demons, diseases, curses and bondages. One who has slept with many people has many soul ties. This explains the reason why some people become more and more promiscuous. When you keep divorcing and remarrying, you entangle yourself with many persons. This affects your marital life and your family. If you want a stable marriage, you must deal with the soul ties that you have established in the past. How many sexual partners have you had in the past? What have you done to liberate your soul?

6. Soul ties with the dead
"David covered his face and cried with a loud voice, "O my son Absalom, O Absalom, my son, my son!" And Joab came into the house, and said to the king, "You have shamed this day the faces of all your servants......for I perceive

that if Absalom had lived, and we all had died, then it would have pleased you well." (2 Sam 19:4-6)

King David had an unhealthy soul tie with his son, Absalom, who rebelled against him and contributed to the deaths of thousands. David's tie was undoubtedly rooted in guilt, for in many ways he had failed in the raising of the young man. The result being that after Absalom was killed and his armies routed, David shamed his own armies by his obsession.

You must be careful not to mourn a dead loved one to an extent that you lose your motivation to press on in life. When someone you love dies, what you should do is that when the mourning period comes to an end, pray and break every soul tie you had with him/her because life must continue. It is foolish to make vows to a corpse like – I will never marry again because I love you. Some people always dream and see themselves fellowshipping with their dead loved ones. Break the soul tie if you are in such a situation. If you cannot help yourself, go for deliverance.

The same thing can happen with women who have had an abortion. Even after they've asked and received forgiveness for the deed, guilt and shame often remain. This is generally an indication of a soul tie with the aborted child. Until and unless the soul tie is broken, the mother will be subject to attacks of depression and guilt. But when that bond is cut off, they're able to put it behind them once and for all, and live life free from the failure of their past.

7. Soul ties with the demonic
"Cleave unto the Lord as you have done this day....take good heed that you love the Lord your God. Else if you do turn back and cleave unto these ungodly nations...then know that the Lord will no more drive them out; but they will be snares and traps to you, scourges in your sides and thorns in your eyes, until you perish from off this good land which the Lord has given you." (Jeremiah 23:8-13)

The prophet plainly warns Israel here that if they "cleave" to the demonic nations around them instead of "cleaving" to God, then the Lord will let them reap what they sow. Any and all involvement with idolatry, witchcraft or the occultism will result in soul ties with evil spirits. That's because such involvement is in direct opposition to the first commandment,

"Thou shall not have any gods before me."
(Exodus 20:3-5)

Some people are struggling with spiritual problems today because of demonic soul ties that were through their exposure to occultism, witchcraft or idol worship.

Steps to Breaking Ungodly Soul Ties

1. Identify all unhealthy soul ties in your life and write them down.
2. Repent from your heart for violating God's ordained boundaries in your relationships. Ask God to forgive you for opening up to unhealthy soul ties.
3. Identify and write down the names of people you are bound to in an ungodly manner that you must separate from. Make a solemn commitment to the Lord to break off these unholy relationships.
4. Become accountable to others to help you keep that commitment.
5. Destroy or throw away any object that can rekindle that ungodly relationship (pictures, gifts, etc.)

212

Until you do the above, any prayers for freedom are in vain. Reinforce your requests to the Lord with a commitment to obey His will. Before praying, always do whatever is necessary for the anointing of the Holy Spirit to come. This is so important. Pray, wait, forgive, or worship. Once His presence and anointing is present, then proceed with the soul tie breaking prayers. It's the anointing that breaks the yoke. The ties won't break with a simple prayer from the mind. The anointed power of the Holy Spirit must be present to be effective.

PRAYER POINTS

1. *Thank God for divine revelation and for the grace of a new beginning that is coming on your life and family.*
2. *Worship God because He is able to change your situation and make you to become the person He wants.*
3. *Thank God for exposing soul ties in your life and family that must be dealt with.*
4. *Thank and worship God for the price paid for your total deliverance on the cross.*
5. *Thank God for the blessings He has made available for you in Christ Jesus.*
   Place your right hand on your chest as you pray these prayers.

6. *Father God I repent for allowing this unhealthy soul tie of (name sin).*

7. *I repent of the sin of idolatry, of allowing this relationship with .... (mention names) to become a hindrance in my life with you.*

8. *I forgive ..... (person with whom soul tie was made) for their part in making and strengthening this unhealthy soul tie.*

9. *I break this soul tie in the Name of Jesus and renounce every unholy part of the bond.*

10. *In the mighty name of Jesus, I break any hold that demons have in this soul tie.*

11. *In the mighty name of Jesus, I command every demon behind these soul ties to pack out of my life for good.*

12. *I call back every emotion, thought and part of my will that was given to ... (call the name) and I give back every emotion, thought and part of his/her will that was imparted on me.*

13. *I receive the healing anointing for the restoration of my soul in the name of Jesus.*

14. *In the mighty name of Jesus, I command every cloud of demonic manipulation over my mind to scatter by fire.*

15. *In the mighty name of Jesus, I break any spiritual rope tying me to ...... (name).*

16. *I break any soul tie I have with the dead .... (name) in the name of Jesus.*

17. Let the fountain of the blood of Jesus purify me body soul and spirit.

18. Let every soul tie with ungodly friends be broken in the mighty name of Jesus.

19. Lord, connect me to the right type of friends in Jesus' name.

20. Let every unhealthy soul ties with my parents and family members be scatter in the name of Jesus.

21. Lord, give me grace to keep healthy relationships with my family members in the name of Jesus.

22. I the mighty name of Jesus I command every soul tie with any occultic or witchcraft kingdom to scatter by fire.

23. In the mighty name of Jesus, I command any yoke of human manipulation on my life to be broken.

24. O Lord, renew my mind and give me the mind of Christ.

25. Let all open doors to demonic manipulations through evil soul ties in my life be closed by the blood of Jesus.

26. Prophesy on your life. See chapter 6.

DAY 22:
DESTROYING EVIL SPIRITUAL MARRIAGES

What is An Evil Spiritual Marriage?

An evil spiritual marriage is situation where a human being is spiritually entangled with demonic spirits (succubus and incubus spirits). The subject of the evil spiritual marriage has been grossly misunderstood by many people. While some hold erroneous views, others demonstrate partial knowledge of this all- important subject. From personal experience in the deliverance ministry I have come to understand that some people are actually married spiritually – some consciously and some unconsciously.

Wicked Activities of the Incubus and the Succubus Spirits

1. Sexual harassments in dreams

The succubus spirit is usually called "the spirit wife" while the incubus spirit is called "the spirit husband." These spirits come to have sexual intercourse with their victims when they are asleep.

216

2. Control and destruction

They also try to control and rule their victims, resulting to: broken marriages, serious gynecological problems, marital distress, miscarriages and impotence. These spirits have destroyed marriages more than any other power.

3. Stagnation and hardship

Those with evil spiritual marriages go through: untold hardship, financial failure and general failure at the edge of breakthrough. In fact, studies show that many people in the church are affected by these spirits. Unfortunately, many are ignorant. Get the truth and be free in the name of Jesus.

"Therefore my people are gone into captivity, because they have no knowledge: and their honorable men are famished, and their multitude dried up with thirst." (Isa 5:13).

You must know that the supernatural world is as real as the physical. What takes place in the spiritual realm affects us physically in our day to day lives.

How Evil Spiritual Marriages are Established

1. Sinful sexual unions

All sexual unions that are condemned by the Bible are open doors to the spirits of incubus and succubus – fornication, adultery, incest, homosexuality, orgies, sadism, bestiality, lesbianism, rape and others.

2. Perversion

The following perverse activities will open your life to the spirits of incubus and succubus: masturbation, pornography, listening to immoral music, watching indecent movies, sensual dressing and use of indecent language.

3. Parental dedication by initiation, incision, idol worship

Most idolatrous parents innocently initiate their children to the idols they worship for protection, prosperity, longevity and knowledge. When these rites are performed with articles and blood of an animal with incision made, it become terrible blood covenants, tying their children to those idols legally. The spirits behind those idols begin to rule those children. Sometimes delay in childbearing leads people to involve themselves with witchdoctors. Children born after those rituals are performed end up entangled.

4. Inherited sins or evil foundations

The transference of sexual sins, for instance with the spirit of inheritance through the (maternal or paternal) blood line opens the door for the spirit of Asmodee (the prince of lust) and the agents, spirit husbands/wives to enter the offspring. In fact, this door of inheritance is opened for incubi and succubae to swim in.

5. Occult participation and involvement

Anyone involved in any occultic practices is exposed to these spirits. Any person whose parents participate in occults has a high exposure rate to attack of demons and manipulation. Such parents initiate their children (born and unborn) by proxy. Such names so initiated enter into occult "computers" where demons are allocated to such personalities. Certain dubious friends and relations can initiate others by proxy – in their absence. (Read Deut.18:10-12).

6. Cultural dances

If you ever got involve with cultural entertainment and dancing either in the village or in an urban area, you have probably got involved with a spiritual altars. If you dance before such idols you might become a bride or a bridegroom to them. (Read Exo.32:5-6).

7. Unprofitable gifts

Another way of being entangled with spiritual marriage is through the acceptance of unprofitable gifts. Today, many people are unconsciously married to spirit husband and spirit wives because they collected certain gifts. If you receive cheap gifts from people, you may be, collecting objects of initiation into ungodly spiritual marriages.

8. Inheriting satanic priesthood

An average African family has a family idol or shrine. These idols are generally inherited from our ancestors. Some of the idols have been worshipped by generations for hundreds of years. Because we live in a modern age, many of those idols have been destroyed or thrown away but the links with them are not yet broken.

Families that have idols also have priests who minister to their idols. What does "priest" mean? It basically means marriage to a deity. So those who have been chosen to serve these idols are bound by the spirits behind the idols. This is the reason why some people have evil spiritual marriages.

Some Symptoms of Evil Spiritual Marriage

If you have been experiencing the following symptoms it is likely that you are entangled in a spiritual marriage:

1. Continuous marital distresses (constant disagreements, quarrelling and fighting);
2. Constant sexual relationships in dreams. Sometimes on and off;
3. Hatred of marriage (refusal to marry whosoever);
4. Strong uncontrollable sexual desires;
5. Divorce and remarriage;
6. Neglect or abandonment by your spouse (sometimes for no serious reason);
7. Demonic dream assistance (some strange person always giving you help in the dream);
8. Swimming or seeing a river in the dream (marriage with the marine kingdom);
9. Missing one's menstrual period in the dream regularly;

221

10. Pregnancy in the dream on regular basis;
11. Breast- feeding a baby in the dream from time to time;
12. Shopping with a strange man or a woman in the dream;
13. Seeing a strange man or woman sleeping by your side in the dream
14. Hatred by your spouse;
15. Serious gynecological problems;
16. Having a miscarriage or falling sick after sexual intercourse in dreams;
17. Constantly wedding in dreams;
18. You always feel the presence of an invisible person with you;
19. A voice tells you that you cannot marry (sometimes in your thoughts or in your dreams).

Steps to Freedom

1. Repent from every sin you have identified.
2. Put away any sexual partner that is not your spouse.
3. Break the soul tie.
4. Destroy any pornographic materials in your keeping.
5. Destroy any idol, charm or occultic materials.
6. Prayer and fasting. Pray until you are free.

7. In case you cannot handle it, meet a godly deliverance minster for assistance.

PRAYER POINTS
Pray these prayers aloud. Do not stop even if there is a strange manifestation in you.

1. Prayer for the anointing
I ask for the presence of God to over shadow me now as the dew of Hermon and His anointing oil, which breaks the yokes, to fall on my head and run through me to work out a great deliverance. As it is written, it has to pass today that the burden of the spirit husband/ wife shall be take off my shoulders and his/her yoke off my neck and the yoke shall be destroyed by the reason of the anointing oil in the mighty name of Jesus Christ.

2. Prayer of Declaration of faith
By the grace of God, I have accepted Jesus Christ and I am now saved. Jesus loves me, he shed his blood for me and washed me in that same blood, brought me back from the hand of my strong enemy and redeemed me. I am a beneficiary of every work of redemption and restoration which Jesus finished on the cross of Calvary through death Jesus destroyed him who had the power

223

death. Now, I shall not die but live because Jesus has become my deliverer, my defender, my protector, my high tower, my refuse, my victory, the author and the finisher of my faith. Jesus has set me free and I have received deliverance. I have been delivered from the law of sin and death. God has translated my life from the kingdom of darkness into the kingdom of his dear own son.

3. Prayer to cancel every evil spiritual marriage

In the name of Jesus, let every spiritual dowry ever paid on me by the spirit husband/wife be made of no effect again in my life by the blood of Jesus Christ. Let any legal ground in the form of agreement, promises, vows and covenants made on my behalf be canceled by the blood of Jesus Christ. I renounce and reject any marriage ring or any token given to me by that spirit wife/husband in the name of Jesus. I break every rule and law binding me to him/ her with the blood of Jesus. I set on fire any wedding certificate, wedding ring, gown and gifts. Let every spirit child that is between be roasted by fire now, in the name of Jesus. Let the blood of Jesus that cleanses from all impurities purge my body, soul and spirit of every sexual pollution and contamination of the spirit husband/ wife.

4. Prayer to break evil marriage covenants

Every covenant that is strongly binding me to any evil spiritual marriage be broken now! For it is written, God has made a new covenant with me in the blood of Jesus Christ and all others are old and annulled. Every curse place upon my body, my business, my property, my home and marriage by the sprit husband/wife loose your hold now by the blood of Jesus. Who shall curse him that the Lord has blessed. From today I am blessed and no curse shall abide on me again in the mighty name of Jesus.

Lay your right hand on your abdomen and continue to pray violently:

1. *Every spirit wife/ every spirit husband, die, in the name of Jesus.*
2. *Everything you have deposited in my life, come out by fire, in the name of Jesus.*
3. *Every power that is working against my marriage, scatter, in the name of Jesus.*
4. *I divorce and renounce my marriage with the spirit husband or wife, in the name of Jesus.*
5. *I break all covenants entered into with the spirit husband or wife, in the name of Jesus.*
6. *I command the thunder fire of God to burn to ashes the wedding gown, ring, photographs and*

225

all other materials used for the marriage, in Jesus' name.

7. I send the fire of God to burn to ashes the marriage certificate, in the name of Jesus.

8. I break every blood and soul-tie covenants with the spirit husband or wife, in the name of Jesus.

9. I send thunder fire of God to burn to ashes the children born to the marriage, in Jesus' name.

10. I withdraw my blood, sperm or any other part of my body deposited on the altar of the spirit husband or wife, in Jesus name.

11. You spirit husband or wife tormenting my life and earthly marriage I bind you with hot chains and fetters of God and cast you out of my life into the deep pit, and I command you not to ever come into my life again, in the name of Jesus.

12. I return to you, every property of yours in my possession in the spirit world, including the dowry and whatsoever was used for the marriage and covenants, in the name of Jesus.

13. I drain myself of all evil materials deposited in my body as a result of our sexual relation, in Jesus' name.

14. Lord, send Holy Ghost fire into my root and burn out all unclean things deposited in it by the spirit husband or wife, in the name of Jesus.

15. I break the head of the snake, deposited into my body by the spirit husband or wife to do me harm,

and command it to come out, in the name of Jesus.

16. I purge out, with the blood of Jesus, every evil material deposited in my womb to prevent me from having children on earth.

17. Lord, repair and restore every damage done to any part of my body and my earthly marriage by the spirit husband or wife, in the name of Jesus.

18. I reject and cancel every curse, evil pronouncement, spell, jinx, enchantment and incantation place upon me by the spirit husband or wife, in the name of Jesus.

19. I take back and possess all my earthly belonging in the custody of the spirit husband or wife, in Jesus' name.

20. I command the spirit husband or wife to turn his or her back on me forever, in Jesus' name.

21. I renounce and reject the name given to me by the spirit husband or wife, in the name of Jesus.

22. I hereby declare and confess that the Lord Jesus Christ is my Husband for eternity, in Jesus' name.

23. I soak myself in the blood of Jesus and cancel the evil mark or writings placed on me, in Jesus' name.

24. I set myself free from the stronghold, domineering power and bondage of the spirit husband or wife, in the name of Jesus.

25. I paralyze the remote control power and work used to destabilize my earthly marriage and to hind me from bearing children for my earthly husband or wife, in the name of Jesus.

26. I announce to the heavens that I am forever married to Jesus.

27. Every trademark of evil marriage be shaken out of my life, in the name of Jesus.

28. I declare myself a virgin for the Lord, in Jesus' name.

29. Let every evil veil upon my life be torn open, in Jesus' name.

30. O Lord, restore all marriages that have been destroyed by the spirit of succubus and incubus in the name of Jesus.

DAYS 23-24:
SPIRITUAL REVIVAL IN THE
CHURCH AND THE NATION

Read: *Acts 19: 1-22, Isaiah 64: 1-5, Hosea 10: 12-13*

True spiritual revival is God amongst His people revealing His holiness, mercy and power. As Peter C. Wagner says, "an authentic spiritual revival is the result of a deep out pour of the Holy Spirit in the lives of those who have been regenerated by Him according to their faith in Christ as Lord". When the early Church sought God and His presence was released on them, both their spiritual and physical needs were met. We desperately need God in the Church in this nation today. The Church is becoming very broad but only a few inches deep. People commit sin but are still very bold to stand and minister before God's people. We have preachers who say that they are not called to preach on sin but on prosperity. The world is becoming churchy, while the church is fast becoming worldly. There is hope; God is sending a revival in answer to our earnest prayers.

Many believers who are conversant with God's prophetic agenda for Cameroon know that there is a mighty spiritual revival that is coming to Cameroon. Read my book, *"Your Time for Divine Expansion: A prophetic Message to the Church in Cameroon"*.

In the seventies a man of God called Steve Lightle visited Cameroon from Braunschweig Germany. He came because during a prayer meeting with a group of believers they had seen a vision of the map of Africa shining. The light source was Cameroon. Many other startling prophecies make it clear that God has a great plan for our nation. This great revival that will shake Cameroon and flow out to other nations will come through labor in prayer. We must sanctify ourselves and begin to seek God. The burden to fast for 30 days every year was born in my heart from this vision of the forth Coming revival in Cameroon. I am still believing God for this great revival. I want you to consecrate your life so that God can prepare you to become an instrument in this coming revival.

As we wait for this mighty revival let's commit ourselves to pray, preach and live the gospel. Your reward in heaven shall depend on how much you have labored here on earth for the advancement of the kingdom of God. The kingdom of God here is not primarily church buildings but the lives of men transformed into the image of Christ. The question is, how many souls have you brought to the Lord since you were born again? How much of all your wealth have you transferred already into your heavenly account through supporting the gospel? How is your Christian life? How rooted are you in the Holy Scriptures? Today, I challenge you to be a Christian indeed, bear in mind that it is not about your denomination but about Christ.

PRAYER POINTS

1. *Lord, thank you for today and for our beloved nation Cameroon. (Take time and worship God for all He has invested in Cameroon and for what He is doing in this nation).*

2. *Plead with God to forgive Cameroon for the sins of corruption, rejection of the gospel, homosexuality, lesbianism, occultism, witchcraft, idol worship, evil traditions, human sacrifices, prostitution, crime, bribery, tribalism, confidence in self, drunkenness, killing, etc.*

3. *Ask God to purify the land with the blood of Jesus.*

4. *Renounce every satanic covenant our leaders have made with occult societies.*

5. *Ask the blood of Jesus to speak on behalf of Cameroon, nullifying every claim Satan holds against us.*

6. *O Lord, release the fire of judgment against all forces of darkness oppressing our leadership.*

7. *O Lord, release your hand against demonic powers oppressing our economy.*

8. *Lord, release the spirit of conviction on the nation of Cameroon.*

9. *Let prison doors of sin open for the salvation of Cameroonians in Jesus' name.*

10. *O Lord, pour your Spirit afresh on the Church in Cameroon.*

11. *O Lord, forgive the Church in Cameroon for being indifferent.*

12. *Lord, forgive the evil and wickedness that is going on in the Churches that is hindering unbelievers to change.*

13. *O Lord, pour out the Spirit of aggressive prayer on all the Christians in every denomination.*

14. *Lord, pour out the Spirit of righteousness and the fear of God on all the Christians.*

15. *O Lord, do a work of sanctification in the Churches.*

16. *Let there be a rapid spiritual growth in your Church in Cameroon in Jesus' name.*

17. *O Lord, let the Church grow in number in Jesus' name.*

18. O Lord, restore unity in the Churches in Jesus' name.
19. Lord, cause Christians from different denominations to be united.
20. O Lord, release a mighty anointing for signs and wonders in the Churches in Jesus' name.
21. We break every veil of religion over the people in Jesus' name.
22. Lord, send revival among the Catholics, Moslems, Jehovah witnesses etc.
23. O Lord, send grace for financial prosperity in the Churches in Cameroon.
24. O Lord, the let the Churches not be distracted from the mission of the Church which is missions.
25. Arise O Lord, let the forces of darkness gathered against the Church in Cameroon be scattered in Jesus' name.
26. We pull down every occult power invoked against the Church in Jesus' name.
27. We command the heavens to be open over the Church in Cameroon in Jesus' name.
28. O Lord, create a spirit of humility and brokenness among the believers.
29. O Lord, reveal to believers the depth and the evil of their sins in Jesus' name.
30. O Holy Spirit, move on the believers and cause them to confess and repent of their sins.

31. O Lord, grant the believers hunger for your word and a readiness to obey it in Jesus' name.

32. Dear Holy Spirit, stir within every believer a desire to search and to know the Word of God.

33. O Lord, cause every believer to be a doer of the Word and not simply a hearer of the Word.

34. Lord, reveal anything that is not pleasing to you in our Church in Jesus' name

35. O Lord, remove anything that is hindering the Church from experiencing a genuine working of the Holy Spirit in revival in Jesus' name.

36. O Lord, fill the members with a burning desire to fast, pray and share the good news with the lost.

37. O Lord, give the believers a deeper love for the Lord Jesus Christ.

38. Merciful God release the angels of goodness and mercy to defend the Church by day and by night.

39. O Lord, prosper and establish every member in righteousness in Jesus' name.

DAYS 25-26:
WAR AGAINST IDOLS

When I was preparing to begin writing this book, the Lord spoke to me very clearly concerning the condition of many people – individuals and families. He showed me a dark cloud hanging over many people. He told me that the cloud was the result of centuries of idolatry. Because of the cloud many are languishing under poverty, diseases, divorces, and immorality. He told me that the reason why some people cannot persevere in the Christian faith, some are very poor and miserable, and some who have been called into ministry cannot serve well is the negative effects of idolatry. He said until this dark cloud is broken over individuals, families and the land many ministries will not excel, some families will continue to agonize, and many destinies will not be fulfilled. So the war against idolatry is very urgent and severe. We must arise and fight until there is a mighty release of God's river of restoration in our lives, families and the land.

What is an Idol?

The Encarta Dictionary gives three meanings of the word "idol": somebody or something greatly admired or loved, often to excess; something that is worshipped as a god, e.g. a statue or carved image and an object of worship other than the one true God. Biblically, an idol is anything that has occupied God's place in the life of a human being.

Types of Idols

1. Personal Idols
Some people have statues, trees, stones, rings, bags, etc. as personal idols. They go to these idols to do incantations or offer sacrifices. Some of these idols are stationed in one place while others are carried around.

2. Personal Modern Idols
Anything or somebody you greatly admire or love to excess is an idol in this category. These people or things occupy God's place in your life. Examples are: sports, games, sports stars, music and music stars, material possessions, sex, alcohol, tobacco, drugs, the only child you have, etc.

"Therefore put to death your members which are on the earth: fornication, uncleanness, passion,

**evil desire, and covetousness, which is idolatry."
(Col.3:5).**

Family Idols

Most families in this nation have their family idols. Family members gather occasionally to offer sacrifices to these idols. Usually these idols are either representations of some gods or the ancestors. Examples: sacred trees, family shrines, stones, skulls of the dead, snakes, statues, graves, rivers, etc. The families that have such idols have priests who serve them.

Tribal and national idols

Every village in our nation has their idols. Seasonally the villagers gather there to offer sacrifices to their ancestors. In some cases the chief priests go on behalf of the whole tribe. Some nations have their national idols (gods).

23 Terrible Consequences of Idolatry

I want you to know that any form of idolatry is a gross violation of God's commandments. God has commanded us not to own or worship any type of idol.

237

"I am the LORD your God . . . You shall have no other gods before Me. You shall not make for yourself a carved image, or any likeness of anything that is in heaven above, or that is in the earth beneath, or that is in the water under the earth; you shall not bow down to them nor serve them. For I, the LORD your God, am a jealous God, visiting the iniquity of the fathers on the children to the third and fourth generations of those who hate Me," (Ex.20:2-5)

1. Idolatry provokes God to jealousy (Ex.20:5).
2. Idolatry attracts divine punishment (Ex.20:5).
3. Idolatry brings punishment upon innocent children right to the fourth generation (Ex.20:5).
4. Idolatry will cause God to reject you (1Sam.15:23).
5. Those who turn to idols will suffer what they are running away from (Isa.66:4).
6. Those who turn to idols shall be consumed (Isa.66:17).
7. Idolatry makes people dull-hearted (Jer.10:8).
8. Idol worshipper shall end up in shame and disgrace (Hos.10:6).
9. Idols will cause God to abhor or detest you (Lev.26:30).
10. Those who worship idols are punished with anger (Deut.32:21).

11. Idols provoke God to anger (1Kgs.16:26).
12. Idol worship will cause you to do abominable things (1Kgs.21:26).
13. Idols will cause you to abandon God (2Kgs.17:15).
14. Idols ensnare (entangle) those who worship them (Ps.106:36).
15. Idols will fail in time of trouble (Isa.31:7).
16. Shame, disgrace and confusion follow those who worship idols (Isa.45:16).
17. Double punishment for those who worship idols (Jer.16:18).
18. Idols will cause you to stumble on the way (Jer.18:15).
19. Idol worship causes insanity (madness) (Jer.50:38).
20. Idol worship causes premature death (Eze.6:4-5, 22:4).
21. Idols defile a person (Eze.20:31).
22. Idols will cause God to pour out His fury on the land (Eze.36:18).
23. Idol worship will cause God to raise Hid hand against you (Eze.44:12).

God has not changed His mind concerning idolatry – He still hates it. From the above consequences of idolatry, you can now understand why some individuals, families, tribes and nations are suffering from all sorts of calamities. What people call natural disasters sometimes are divine judgments to punish idolatry.

Spiritual Research Results

The table below shows the results of a scientific research carried out by Dr. D.K. Olukoya during a period of 30 years – sampling 500 ministers of the gospel. It shows the effects of family foundations (background) on the ministry.

Family Background	Failure Rate
1. Ministers who bear the names of the occult (idols)	80%
2. Converted occultists who became 50% ministers	
3. Ministers from riverine areas (those who worship water spirits)	80%
4. Ministers whose parents served Satan (idol priests, witchdoctors, etc.)	90%
5. Ministers who happen to be pastors children	30%
6. Ministers whose parents were possessed	85%
7. Ministers from nominal Christian Parents	60%
8. Ministers who converted from Islam	60%
9. Ministers from polygamous homes	75%
10. Ministers whose parents are born again	9%

How to Deal with Idols

1. Identify them
This is the first step to deal with idolatry. Do a check from personal idols in your to those around you that you must deal with. Also identify the idols of you family, tribe and your nation.

2. Repentance
Ask God to forgive you for involving yourself directly or indirectly. Plead for God's mercy upon your family and tribe.

3. Destroy them
God has commanded us to destroy all idols by fire. He orders us to put to death even the idols of our hearts. **"Therefore put to death your members which are on the earth: fornication, uncleanness, passion, evil desire, and covetousness, which is idolatry." (Col.3:5).**
"But thus you shall deal with them: you shall destroy their altars, and break down their sacred pillars, and cut down their wooden images, and burn their carved images with fire."(Deut.7:5).

4. Commit yourself to God
Dedicate yourself entirely to God. Decide to worship only Him the rest of your life.

**"You shall have no other gods before Me."
(Ex.20:3).
"And you shall love the LORD your God with all
your heart, with all your soul, with all your mind,
and with all your strength." (Mark 12:30).**

Spiritual warfare

Idols have evil spirits masquerading behind them.
Whenever you offer sacrifices to idols, you
fellowship directly with demons.
**"Rather, that the things which the Gentiles
sacrifice they sacrifice to demons and not to God,
and I do not want you to have fellowship with
demons." (1Cor.10:20)**

For you to be free from the covenants that have
been established with the idols, you must engage in
spiritual warfare. The sad thing is that some people
think that they are automatically free because they
have refused to go back to the village for idol
worship. You must receive the new covenant in the
blood of Jesus Christ and use it to break all evil
covenants with the idols. Don't forget that there is
not neutral ground in this matter – you are either
standing on Jesus' victory or exposed to demonic
harassments. Sometimes the demons behind the
idols will try to resist your freedom. You must resist

them in faith, prayer and fasting until the surrender completely.

Labor for the deliverance of your family, community, tribe and nation

It is the responsibility of all those who have experienced deliverance from idolatry and demonic manipulations to help their family members and communities to see the light too. You have to fast and pray for them. Also look for opportunities to preach to them and share your deliverance experience with them.

All of us must fight the war against idolatry because the negative consequences of idolatry affect everybody. The violence in our society, ritual killings and crime that has its roots in idolatry is affecting everybody. Do not be indifferent at this time that the battle is becoming more serious than ever.

PRAYER POINTS

From your findings make sure that during your prayer, mention the names of the idols and shrines you have identified from your background.

1. *Lord, I thank and praise you for my life and for the blood of Jesus shed for me on the cross.*
2. *Lord, I worship you because you have set me free to the uttermost by the blood of Jesus.*
3. *Lord forgive me for the sins I know and those I do not know.*
4. *O Lord, I repent deeply from all the wicked things our forefathers have done (covenants with demons, innocent bloodshed, unfaithfulness, polygamy, rejection of the gospel, etc.).*
5. *Forgive us and cleanse our families with the precious blood of Jesus Christ.*
6. *In the name of Jesus I denounce the gods of my father's and of my mother's houses.*
7. *I loose myself free from any connection with any family shrine and altar in Jesus' name.*
8. *I cancel every evil contract established between my ancestors and demons in Jesus' name.*
9. *With the blood of Jesus Christ I wipe out all satanic demand, covenants and agreements with my ancestors in Jesus' name.*
10. *In the mighty name of Jesus I cancel all spiritual marriages and dedications established with demons in Jesus' name.*

11. In the mighty name of Jesus I bind every strongman of my family.

12. Every power from my father's house working against me be destroyed in Jesus' name

13. Every evil power from my mother's house be destroyed in Jesus name.

14. Let the shrines of my father's house and of my mother's house receive the fire of judgment in Jesus name.

15. I break the influences of all family gods from my life and those of my children.

16. I break the influences of all family and tribal God's from my life and family in the name of Jesus.

17. Every spirit from my father's/ mother's houses assigned to monitor my life be bound in Jesus' name.

18. I bind any ancestral spirit that is working against my destiny and that of my family in Jesus' name.

19. I pull down the altars of ancestral worship in my family and tribe Jesus' name.

20. I raise an altar of righteousness in my family and my tribe in Jesus' name.

21. Every limit set by the enemy on my way and family, I violate it in Jesus' name.

22. I declare that my family and people from my tribe shall serve the Lord in the name of Jesus.

23. I dedicate my children and even the unborn to God in Jesus' name.

24. Goodness and mercy shall follow my family all the days of our lives in the name of Jesus.

25. O Lord, let the covenant in the blood of Jesus Christ cancel any other covenant in my life.

26. Let every spiritual embargo on my life and destiny be lifted today once and forever.

27. Let every evil effect of these covenants in my life be consumed by fire to ashes.

28. Let every disease in my body and family associated with these evil covenants wither.

29. O Lord, let the mantle of breakthrough fire fall on my body, soul and spirit.

30. Let the mantle of fire fall on my finances and relationships.

31. I break out of every tribal limitation in Jesus' name.

32. From today, what I could not have because of my background, I will have in Jesus' name. Any level I could not attain because of my background, I shall attain by divine favor.

33. Lord, raise vibrant men and women of God from my family and trine in the name of Jesus.

DAYS 27:
BE HEALED!

Read: *Deuteronomy 7: 12-15, Psalm 103:1-5*

God has provided for the healing of all your diseases in the healing covenant established in the blood of Jesus Christ. You can be healed of any type of disease with or without a name.

"Who forgives all your iniquities, Who heals all your diseases" (Psalm103:3)

"If you diligently heed the voice of the LORD your God and do what is right in His sight, give ear to His commandments and keep all His statutes, I will put none of the diseases on you which I have brought on the Egyptians. For I am the LORD who heals you."

God has a covenant of healing with His people. His healing covenant name is *"Jehovah Rapha"* – The LORD who heals (Ex.15:26). A covenant is a mutual understanding between two or more parties, each binding himself to fulfill specified obligations. In the healing covenant deal, God has committed Himself to heal and to spare His covenant children from diseases. On the other hand, the beneficiaries of the covenant must keep all His commandments. By this covenant God became a doctor for the Israelites. He too can become your doctor as you affiliate to the covenant through Jesus Christ.

God is faithful to heal all those who keep the covenant. He did it to the Israelites.
"He also brought them out with silver and gold, And there was none feeble among His tribes." (Ps.105:37).

Because God was their doctor, none of them was feeble. They were strong and vibrant for 40 years in the harsh wilderness. No disease is permitted to kill you as you live in the covenant. (See Ps.10:1-5, Ps.107:17-20, 2Chron.30:1820).

Diseases afflict God's covenant people when they disobey God's commandments. Diverse kinds of diseases that come as a result of this rebellion are recorded in the Bible (see Deut.28:15-29). When God's people repent and seek Him, He heals them.
"If my people, which are called by my name, shall humble themselves, and pray, and seek my face, and turn from their wicked ways; then will I hear from heaven, and will forgive their sin, and will heal their land." (2chron.7:14)

248

God's medicine for your healing in the covenant is His word.

"He sent his word, and healed them, and delivered them from their destructions." (Ps.107:20). The word of God activates faith in the heart of the sick for the healing miracle to take place (Rom.10:17). Man's words provoke fear, doubt and distrust. Open your heart to God's word, keep it in your heart and your healing will come unfailingly (see Prov.4:20-22). Today His word to you is, *"Be healed in the mighty name of Jesus Christ!"*

PRAYER POINTS

(Lay your hand on your body and on those who are sick and pray these prayers)

1. *Lord, thank you for your healing power made available for me on the cross.*
2. *Lord, thank you because I know now that it is your will that I should be healed and also live a healthy life.*
3. *On the grounds of the finished work of the cross I curse every disease in my body to day today in the name of Jesus.*
4. *I command every spirit of infirmity behind this disease to leave my life now in the name of Jesus.*
5. *I receive my total healing from ….. (name the problem) now in the name of Jesus.*

6. I overthrow the citadel of sickness, weakness and fear in my life in the name of Jesus.

7. Let me be transfused with the Blood of the Lord Jesus Christ for divine purification

8. I apply the blood of Jesus on my spirit soul body and my womb.

9. Let the fire of God saturate my womb in the name of Jesus

10. Let every design against my life be completely nullify in the name of Jesus

11. I vomit every satanic deposits in my body in the mighty name of Jesus. (if you feel as to vomit, do so).

12. Let the blood the fire and the living water of the most high God wash my system clean from – Unprofitable growth in the womb – Evil plantations – Evil deposits from spirit husband – Impurities acquired from parent contamination – Evil spiritual consumption – Hidden sicknesses – Remote control mechanism – Physical and spiritual incisions – Satanic poisons – Evil stamps, labels and links in the name of Jesus.

13. Let every area of my life become too hot for any evil to inhabit in the name of Jesus.

14. Evil growth in my life be uprooted in the name of Jesus.

15. Let my body reject every evil inhabitation in the mighty name of Jesus.

16. I break the power of the occult, witchcraft and familiar spirit over my life in the name of Jesus.

17. I pass out any Satan deposit in my intestine in the name of Jesus.

18. I pass out any satanic deposit in my reproductive organ in the name of Jesus.

19. I pass out any satanic deposit in my womb in the name of Jesus.

20. In the name of Jesus I declare before all the forces of darkness Jesus Christ is my Lord over every department of my life.

21. You foreign hand laid on my womb, release me in the name of
Jesus.

22. In the name of Jesus I break and loose myself from all evil curses chains spells jinxes bewitchment, witchcraft, sorcery, which may have being put upon me.

23. Let a creative miracle take place in my womb and reproductive system in the name of Jesus.

24. Father I ask you in the name of Jesus to send out your medical angels to operate any area of my body that needs an operation in the name of Jesus.

25. I bind plunder and render to naught every strong man assigned to my womb, reproductive system and marital life in the name of Jesus.

26. *God who quicken the dead quicken my womb and reproductive system in the name of Jesus*

27. *I release myself from the hold of spirit of sterility, infertility and fear in the name of Jesus.*

28. *All spirits rooted in fornication come out of my womb with all your roots in the mighty name of our Lord Jesus.*

29. *Jehovah Rapha, repair and mend every broken area of my entire life in the name of Jesus.*

30. *Dear Lord Jesus, from today, become my personal physician.*

31. *O Lord, establish a wall of fire around my life and family against diseases in the name of Jesus.*

32. *O Lord, cause your covenant children to enjoy divine health in an outstanding way this year in the name of Jesus.*

33. *O Lord, restore the gifts of divine healing in the church in the name of Jesus.*

DAY 28:
BREAKING THE YOKE OF POVERTY AND STAGNATION

Read: *Exodus 12:31-33, 1Chronicles 4:9-10, Genesis 32:24-32)*

How do you feel when your contemporaries are elevated to the next level while you are left behind? Now imagine being on a spot for over 400 years! For that whole period, the Israelites were tied down by forces they could not challenge. They recorded no form of movement. They kept working as slaves but could not move forward or upwards. At best, they wandered about in circles. They remained on the same spot physically, financially and mentally. They remained underdogs for centuries.

Have you been on the same spot for long? Has it been all motion but no movement? Has your lineage experienced an invisible ceiling over the progress of members of your family? That situation of stagnation shall be broken today in Jesus name. What members of your family could not achieve in previous generations shall be achieved by you in this generation.

253

For your breakthrough to come you have an important role to play. You have to diligently follow the principles that God has revealed to us in His word concerning our prosperity. What I have discovered during all these years as a pastor is that many Christians speak the word of God concerning prosperity but very few actually live by what they speak. The few Christians I have met who diligently practice the word of God have uncountable testimonies of uncommon breakthroughs.

Keys to Break Stagnation and Poverty

1. Surrender to Jesus Christ

Jesus is the way to every divine blessing. In Him curses are lifted up and blessings are released. Bring your shattered life to Him – He will arrange it for you.

"Christ has redeemed us from the curse of the law, having become a curse for us . . . that the blessing of Abraham might come upon the Gentiles in
Christ Jesus" (Gal.3:13-14).

"For you know the grace of our Lord Jesus Christ, that though He was rich, yet for your

sakes He became poor, that you through His poverty might become rich." (2Cor.9:6).

2. **Live a righteous life**

The blessings of God are for those who live righteously. One of the reasons why some people stagnate in life is sin. Put your life in order for a divine visitation.

"He will bless those who fear the LORD, Both small and great." (Ps.115:13).

"For You, O LORD, will bless the righteous; With favor You will surround him as with a shield." (Ps.5:12).

3. **Be Obedient to all His commands**

If God is going to take you to the next level you must be ready to obey Him fully. He is going to give you some instructions that may even be challenging. Obey Him promptly and fully, it shall be well with you.

"Now it shall come to pass, if you diligently obey the voice of the LORD your God, to observe carefully all His commandments which I command you today, that the LORD your God will set you high above all nations of the earth." (Deut.28:1).

"If you are willing and obedient, You shall eat the good of the land" (Isa.1:19).

Give God a tithe of all your income

Your tithe is one tenth of all your income. Tithing is God's kingdom insurance policy for your financial prosperity. Your tithe guarantees an open heaven over your life and keeps devourers and wasters away from your investments.

"Bring all the tithes into the storehouse, That there may be food in My house, And try Me now in this," Says the LORD of hosts, "If I will not open for you the windows of heaven And pour out for you such blessing That there will not be room enough to receive it. "And I will rebuke the devourer for your sakes, So that he will not destroy the fruit of your ground, Nor shall the vine fail to bear fruit for you in the field," Says the LORD of hosts" (Mal.3:10-11).

4. Honor God with all the first fruit of your increase

Honoring God with the first fruit of your increase is a key for the activation of the covenant of prosperity. I personally do not eat my first fruit and as a result I have experienced many miraculous financially breakthroughs.

"Honor the LORD with your possessions, And with the first fruits of all your increase; So your

barns will be filled with plenty, And your vats will overflow with new wine." (Prov.3:9-10).

5. Be aggressively generous

Generosity provokes heaven to remember you. Many people have stagnated because of greed. Abraham received a mighty breakthrough after he welcome and three fed strangers (Gen.18:1-14). God Himself will teach you how to be generous if you are willing to learn.

"There is one who scatters, yet increases more; And there is one who withholds more than is right, But it leads to poverty. The generous soul will be made rich, And he who waters will also be watered himself." (Prov.11:24-25).

6. Serve God and people

Service is a key to divine favor. Sometimes when God wants to bless you, He will test you in the area of service. Abraham who was a very wealthy man stood as a servant while the strangers were eating (Gen.18:1-14). There are people in church today that God has started to bless who feel very big to serve. Please humble yourself and serve the more so that you can continue to grow in the blessings.

7. Recognize parental and spiritual authority

One of the channels God's blessings will flow into your life is the parental channel – your spiritual and biological parents. Learn to provoke the blessings they carry through your submission, services and gifts to them. (Read 2Chron.20:20; Gen.25:1-3; Mat.10:40-41; Num.6:27).

8. Aggressive prayers

Stagnation and poverty is sometimes caused by demons. It takes strategic and aggressive prayers for breakthrough to come. You must be ready to pray like brother Jabez if you must move to the next level. Apart from seeking to please God with all my heart, one of the major keys to my success in ministry is aggressive prayer. I have learnt to take what belongs to me by force in prayer.

"And Jabez called on the God of Israel saying, "Oh, that You would bless me indeed, and enlarge my territory, that Your hand would be with me, and that You would keep me from evil, that I may not cause pain!" So God granted him what he requested." (1Chron.4:10).

Sitting down regretting and blaming people will not change your condition. Get up and take charge of your destiny. Tell the devil enough! is enough! How long shall you be a debtor? How long shall you wallow in fruitless labor? When shall you graduate from a receiver to a giver? Hold God like Jacob and say, "O Lord, I will not let you go until you bless me too." (Read Gen.32:22-28). This is your turning point. When your turning point comes, the enemies who refused to release you for several years will be unable to endure your presence for one second. Pray! Pray! Pray!

PRAYER POINTS

1. *Every arrow of evil delay, fired into my star, scatter by fire, in the name of Jesus.*
2. *Every arrow of backwardness, fired into my star, die, in the name of Jesus.*
3. *Chains of stagnation over my life, break, in the name of Jesus.*
4. *Delay tactics, organized against my destiny, scatter, in the name of Jesus.*
5. *Every yoke of disappointment, scatter, in the name of Jesus.*
6. *Thou power of hard-life and fruitless labor, be broken in the name of Jesus.*
7. *Every power ordained to make me rise and fall, be broken in the name of Jesus.*

8. *Every power of my father's house, delaying my breakthroughs, scatter by fire in the name of Jesus.*

9. *Deep pit, swallowing my blessings, vomit them by fire, in the name of Jesus.*

10. *Cloud of darkness around my breakthroughs, scatter, in the name of Jesus.*

11. *I pull down every stronghold of satanic delay, in the name of Jesus.*

12. *Every strongman assigned against my progress, be arrested and cast of my way, in the name of Jesus.*

13. *Failure and calamity shall not be my identity, in the name of Jesus.*

14. *Every power of stagnation in my life, dry up in the name of Jesus.*

15. *Any book of generational failure, bearing my name, catch fire, in the name of Jesus.*

16. *I decree failure is not my portion, in the name of Jesus.*

17. *Every altar of poverty in my place of birth, working against my prosperity, burn to ashes, in Jesus name.*

18. *Today, I raise up altar of continuous prosperity upon my destiny, in the name of Jesus.*

19. *Every stronghold of mental and spiritual poverty in my life, be uprooted by fire, in the name of Jesus.*

20. *Any covenant in my life that is strengthening the stronghold of poverty, break, in the name of Jesus.*

21. *O Lord, create opportunities for my prosperity today, in the name of Jesus.*

22. *I bind and I cast out, every negative word enforcing poverty into my life, in the name of Jesus.*

23. *Spirit of stinginess; disappear from my life, in the name of Jesus.*

24. *I bind and I cast out, the spirit of disobedience, in the name of Jesus.*

25. *Every evil power, sitting on my prosperity, summersaults and scatter, in the name of Jesus.*

DAY 29:
ANOINTING FOR EXPLOITS

Read: *Isaiah 11:1-4, Exodus 31:1-5*

God wants you to be a success in all you do. He had ordained an inheritance for you before you were created. He wants to anoint you to take possession of this inheritance in this season. The question you may ask is, "What is this anointing we are talking about?" The word "anointing" in both the Old and the New Testament speaks of rubbing with oil. In Bible times those who were being ordained into any spiritual office received this anointing with oil. The rubbing of oil symbolized the release of the Holy Spirit on the life of that person. So, in simple terms, we can define the anointing as the power of the Holy Spirit on the life of believer for service. Or divine empowerment for the accomplishment of divine assignments.

Every assignment in God's kingdom has an anointing for its accomplishment. Jesus Christ is one that had the greatest kingdom assignment to accomplish here on earth. The Bible says that He was anointed without measure (John 3:34). It was by the power of this anointing that Jesus did everything – prayer, fasting, preaching, teaching, healing the sick, casting out demons, performing miracles and resisting the enemies of the gospel. Without the anointing He should have failed in His earthly mission.

I want you to know that if Jesus Christ the Son of God who was conceived by the Holy Spirit and who lived a sinless life could not do without the anointing, then you need it more. We want to briefly examine the seven anointings that were on Jesus Christ, which God wants to release on the Church in this season. As you go through them I want you to ask God from your heart to release a fresh anointing on your life. A fresh encounter with the anointing is the key to a life of exploits.

"but the people who know their God shall be strong, and carry out great exploits." (Dan.11:32).

The 7 Anointings (Isa.11:1-3)

1. The Spirit of the LORD
"The Spirit of the LORD shall rest upon Him" (Isa.11:2).

"The Spirit of the LORD" speaks of the authority for government that was on Jesus Christ.

"For unto us a Child is born, Unto us a Son is given; And the government will be upon His shoulder. And His name will be called Wonderful, Counselor, Mighty God, Everlasting Father, Prince of Peace. Of the increase of His government and peace There will be no end, Upon the throne of David and over His kingdom, To order it and establish it with judgment and justice From that time forward, even forever. The zeal of the LORD of hosts will perform this." (Isa.9:6-7)

This is the anointing for spiritual leadership – the type of leadership that glorifies God. The Church urgently needs spiritual leaders who will move God's people from the wilderness to the Promised Land, from spiritual babies to sons of God and from misery to abundance. Every believer is a leader in a particular capacity. This implies that all of us need this anointing.

2. The Spirit of Wisdom

Jesus Christ fulfilled His earthly ministry in the wisdom of God. The Bible calls Him the wisdom of God.
"but to those who are called, both Jews and Greeks, Christ the power of God and the wisdom of God." (1Cor.1:24).

We can see the manifestation of divine wisdom in all He did. He was a creative teacher, a wise leader and one who could easily handle any challenge that came up. For instance, when he was faced with the problem of feeding thousands of people in the wilderness without food the Bible says, **"But this He said to test him, for He Himself knew what He would do." (John 6:6).**

One of the Gifts of the Holy Spirit heaven has made available for all believers is the gift of wisdom (1Cor.12:8). The commands every believer should desperately seek for wisdom because it is the most important thing in life (Prov.4:7). This implies that the anointing for divine wisdom is available for you. This is the same anointing that rested upon King Solomon, Daniel and Joseph. By virtue of the wisdom that was on them they became indispensable assets for their generations and not liabilities. God wants to anoint you with supernatural wisdom to solve complicated human problems. God does not come down Himself to resolve human problems; He empowers dedicated men and women with supernatural abilities to do so. Just look around and see the wonders that the unregenerated brains of men are doing in the world then imagine what the wisdom of God can do through you. It is an insult for a child of God, inhabited by Christ "the wisdom and the power of God" to be a failure. I believe that there should be a supernatural touch on whatsoever vocation or profession you are involved because of the anointing of divine wisdom that is on your life. If this is not yet happening, turn to God today as ask Him to anoint you with divine wisdom.

3. The Spirit of Understanding

The word "understanding" means the ability to grasp meaning, deep knowledge of a particular something or the ability to interpret something. Jesus Christ needed an anointing of understanding upon His life to be able to clearly execute God's mission of salvation in this world.

No doubt He did his work error free.

"Through wisdom a house is built, And by understanding it is established;" (Prov.24:3).

Without this understanding that comes from God you will be far from executing God's will for your life and others. The Bible warns us not to trust on our own understanding (Prov.3:5). One of the major problems of the church today is lack of understanding. The type of things some Christians do would reveal that they are void of the understanding of God's word. It is for this reason that the God is releasing a fresh anointing of understanding on the Church in this season.

4. The Spirit of Counsel

Jesus also had this anointing upon His life. Why do you think God gave Him such an anointing? The answer is found in the meaning of the word "counsel." The word in Hebrews is "*etsah*" and it means advice, plan, prudence and purpose. This anointing ensured that Jesus followed the plan of salvation strictly. It was by this anointing that Jesus understood exactly what step to take in the face of every challenge.

"Where there is no counsel, the people fall; But in the multitude of counselors there is safety." (Prov.11:14).

God wants to anoint you with this grace so that you can fulfill your destiny. He is raising anointed counselors for the Church – men and women who know the mind of God. It is by this anointing that Daniel became the king's counselor in Babylon. May God raise you to become a wise counselor even for your government.

5. The Spirit of Might

"The Spirit of the LORD is upon Me, Because He has anointed Me To preach the gospel to the poor; He has sent Me to heal the brokenhearted, To proclaim liberty to the captives And recovery of sight to the blind, To set at liberty those who are oppressed;" (Luke 4:18).

It was by this anointing that Jesus cast out demons and subdued the kingdom of darkness wherever He went.

The Jesus made it clear that that same power will come on the Church in our days.

"But you shall receive power when the Holy Spirit has come upon you; and you shall be witnesses to Me in Jerusalem, and in all Judea and Samaria, and to the end of the earth." (Acts 1:8).

So if there is power made available for you to walk in dominion, why go about empty. Why allow the demons keep messing your life when you should subdue them and help others too gain their freedom? That nonsense must stop! Fresh fire is coming on your life this season. You will take your place on top and never under again.

6. The Spirit of Knowledge

Jesus Christ – the creator needed anointing while on this planet to express the knowledge of God. By this anointing He knew all He was supposed to know and He also dispensed divine knowledge accurately.

"But Jesus did not commit Himself to them, because He knew all men, and had no need that anyone should testify of man, for He knew what was in man." (John 2:24-25).

One of the gifts of the Holy Spirit God has made available to the Church is the word of knowledge (1Cor.12:8). This gift empowers the believer with a supernatural ability to know hidden things. We need this gift in the church today to be able to expose the hidden works of the enemy. We live in the age of great deceptions. Ask God to fill you with this anointing of divine knowledge.

The Church in this generation needs a touch of God to really know Him. There is a prophecy we must pray that it be fulfilled in our times.

"For the earth will be filled With the knowledge of the glory of the LORD, As the waters cover the sea." (Hab.2:14).

7. The Spirit of the Fear of the LORD

The main reason why Jesus Christ came to this world was to reconcile man to God and to show mankind how to sustain a permanent relationship with God. This is the reason why He needed the anointing of the fear of the LORD.

In the last days God is pouring out the Spirit of the Fear of the LORD afresh on the Church to prepare His children for the rapture. The Bible has revealed that the end time Church is going to face many spiritual challenges, one of which is apostasy. Today we have people who are living in open sin ministering before God's people. Scandals among Christians as well as ministers of the gospel are multiplying every day. Sometimes you hear things that provoke headaches and the question I used to ask is "where is the fear of God?" We need this anointing on our lives in order to serve God and make it to heaven. If you become the most successful minister of your generation or the wealthiest man that has ever lived but lack holiness, you shall NEVER see heaven.

"Pursue peace with all people, and holiness, without which no one will see the Lord:" (Heb.12:14).

Preachers of the gospel need to reemphasize this Bible verse over and over. In our times it is like some people have already made up their minds that they want to go to hell through the Church. Emphasizing a scripture like this one can snatch such people from the yawning mouth of hell.

A rod out of the broken tree
"And there will come a rod out of the broken tree of Jesse, and a branch out of his roots will give fruit." (Isa.11:1) BBE

Jesus Christ was born at the time when the great family of King David had become a very negligible one among the children of Israel. The Babylonian captivity had cut down the family tree along the years. But the miracle is that the stump still produced a shoot (branch) that gave fruits. The Bible speaks first of a "rod out of the broken tree." The rod is "choter" in Hebrews which speaks of a twig or weak shoot. This rod "choter" shall become a branch which will give fruit. The branch is "netser" which means greenness as a striking color or descendant. Though the beginning is small the end shall be great.

You are a rod (a small; negligible twig) that is despised but God has chosen you to bring hope to your family and your generation. It doesn't matter how badly the devil has cut down your family, through you, there is going to be divine restoration. Some people have been mourning for long and blaming their background for their predicaments. It is true that your background or your foundation can hamper your progress but when the anointing comes on you, there is renewal. The anointing raises prince s from the dung hill, it turns slaves to kings, it turns goats to sheep and it transforms persecutors to preachers. It doesn't matter what has been going wrong with your life, receive the anointing today for a turn around.

How to receive and sustain the anointing

1. A right standing with God
2. A hunger for the anointing (you must ask)
3. A spirit of generosity
4. Prayer and fasting
5. A life of humility
6. A life of Obedience
7. Living by faith

PRAYER POINTS
1. *Worship and praise God for the anointing He has made available for you.*

2. *Identify the areas of your life that you need the anointing and start to present them to God.*

3. *Take time and worship God as you open your heart for the anointing. The Lord will fill you to the overflow.*

4. *Pray these prophetic and warfare prayers concerning your life and destiny.*

5. *I command the stronghold of inherited poverty, in my life, to be pulled down by the blood of Jesus.*

6. *Every stigma of poverty in my life, be robbed-off, by the blood of Jesus, in the name of Jesus.*

7. *Holy Spirit, adjust my life into prosperity, in the name of Jesus.*

8. *Every chain of inherited failures upon my life, break by fire, in the name of Jesus.*

9. *Dear Holy Ghost, arrest on my behalf tonight, every spirit of poverty, in the name of Jesus.*

10. *Let the stubborn strongman of poverty in my place of birth (mention the place), be paralyzed by fire, in Jesus name.*

11. *Every territorial spirit working against my prosperity be chained, in the name of Jesus.*

12. *Every covenant of poverty made by the living or the dead against my prosperity, break, in Jesus name.*

13. *Every arrow of poverty, fired into my life, come out with all your roots, in the name of Jesus.*

14. *Every curse of poverty, placed upon my family, be consumed by fire, in the name of Jesus. 14. I receive the mandate to enter into covenant of wealth, in Jesus' name.*

15. *O Lord, anoint me to pluck the seed of wealth that will swallow poverty in my life, in Jesus name.*

16. *From today, my portion in life has changed from a beggar and borrower, to a lender and giver, in Jesus name.*

17. *O Lord, anoint me with the power to lead me to know and do your will.*

18. *Lord, anoint our leaders to minister with power, signs and wonders in the name of Jesus.*

19. *From this day I connect to the fountain of divine knowledge in the name of Jesus.*

20. *O Lord, take away the heart of fear from me and give me the heart of a lion in the name of Jesus.*

21. *O Lord, cause me to operate in the wisdom and power of Jesus Christ who lives in me.*

22. *I refuse to be a disgrace to the Church in my generation. I commit myself to labor in order to bring glory to Jesus' Christ in every area of my life.*

23. *Let the mantle of fire fall on me in the name of Jesus.*

24. *O God of Holiness, restore the anointing of the fear of the Lord in the church.*

25. In the mighty name of Jesus' I refuse to be problem to my generation, I must be a solution in the name of Jesus.
26. I refuse to eat the bread of sorrow, I must enjoy the fruit of my labors in the name of Jesus.
27. I refuse to be a spectator in the house of God, I must touch my generation with the power of God in the name of Jesus.
28. I refuse to be a victim, I must enjoy the victory Jesus has given me on the cross in the name of Jesus.

DAY 30:
THANKSGIVING AND
TESTIMONIES

Read: *Psalm 107; 149; Psalm 150; 40: 1-5*

Today is dedicated to minister to the Lord. You shall not ask anything from Him but praise Him as much as you can for all He has done for you during this time of prayer. The early church understood the power of thanksgiving prayers. They fasted just to minister to God (Thanksgiving and worship).

"As they ministered to the Lord and fasted, the Holy Spirit said, "Now separate to Me Barnabas and Saul for the work to which I have called them" (Acts 13:2).

I want you to know that prayer is like sowing seeds. After the farmer sows the seeds, he waits for the harvest in full assurance. As you wait for the fruit of your prayers to become ripe for harvest, continue praise God. As you praise Him also listen to the leading of the Holy Spirit concerning the next practical steps you have to take from now. Today I also encourage you to give a special thanks giving offering to the Lord to support this ministry. The

Lord is opening more doors for the gospel to be preached. Join us as we spread the fire.

Today is also a day of testimonies. Identify what God has done and begin to share with other people. Your testimony will generate faith in somebody's heart. The Bible reveals that our testimony of salvation is a deadly weapon against the devil. When you testify about what God has done in your life, you give the devil a technical knockout.

"And they overcame him by the blood of the Lamb and by the word of their testimony, and they did not love their lives to the death." (Rev.12: 11)
If you want to always be on top, you must learn to testify.

How can you share you testimonies? Do it in Church, share your testimony during a house fellowship meeting, write an e-mail to a loved one, make a phone call, send an SMS, write it in a Christian newsletter, etc. Do not hide your testimony. Note that the more you testify the more God will give you testimonies.

277

BIBLE READING PLANS

READING THE NEW TESTAMENT IN 30 DAYS:

1. Matthew 1-9
2. Matthew 10-15
3. Matthew 16-22
4. Matthew 23-28
5. Mark 1-8
6. Mark 9-16
7. Luke 1-6
8. Luke 7-11
9. Luke 12-18
10. Luke 19-24
11. John 1-7
12. John 8-13
13. John 14-21
14. Acts 1-7
15. Acts 8-14
16. Acts 15-21
17. Acts 22-28
18. Romans 1-8
19. Romans 9-16
20. 1 Corinthians 1-9
21. 1 Corinthians 10-16
22. Corinthians 1-13
23. Galatians - Ephesians
24. Philippians - 2 Thessalonians
25. 1 Timothy - Philemon
26. Hebrews
27. James - 2 Peter
28. 1 John - 3 John
29. Revelation 1-11
30. Revelation 12-22

READING THE GOSPELS IN 30 DAYS:

1. Matthew 1-4
2. Matthew 5-10
3. Matthew 11-13
4. Matthew 14-16
5. Matthew 17-20
6. Matthew 21-24
7. Matthew 25-28
8. Mark 1-4
9. *Catch Up Day*
10. Mark 5-8

11. Mark 9-12
12. Mark 13-16
13. Luke 1-3
14. Luke 4-7
15. Luke 8-11
16. Luke 12-15
17. Luke 16-17
18. *Catch Up Day*
19. Luke 18-19
20. Luke 20-22

21. Luke 23-24
22. John 1-3
23. John 4-6
24. John 7-10
25. *Catch Up Day*
26. John 8-11
27. John 12-13
28. John 14-16
29. John 17-19
30. John 20-21

SOURCES CONSULTED:

Chavda, Mahesh. *The Hidden Power of Prayer and Fasting*. Shippensburg, PA: Destiny Image Publishers, 1998.

Demonic legal rights, Alive Ministries South Africa, www.aliveministries-sa.org (accessed July 20, 2012).

Godson, Nembo T., *Dealing with Evil Foundations: Power Must Change Hands Vol.1.* Bamenda, Cameroon: Christian Restoration Network Publications, 2011.

Mills, Dag Heward. *Take Up Your Cross: A Call to Sacrifice.* Accra Ghana: Parchment House, 2004.

Moody, Gene B., *The Comprehensive Deliverance Manual.* Baton Rouge, LA: Gene B. Moody Deliverance Ministries, 2002.

Olukoya, D.K, *When the Deliverer Needs Deliverance; Deliverance Manual for Ministers and Church Workers.* Yaba – Lagos: Mountain of Fire and Miracles Ministries Press House, 2007.

Simpson, Chris N., *How and Why Spirits Transfer Between People*: Houston, Texas, 2004. http://www.newwineonline.com (accessed July 20, 2012).

OTHER CHRISTIAN RESTORATION NETWORK PUBLICATIONS:

- ❖ Power Must Change Hands Vol.1: Dealing with Evil
- ❖ Foundations
- ❖ Power Must Change Hands Vol.2: Pursue Overtake and Recover All
- ❖ Power Must Change Hands Vol.3: Jesus Christ Must Reign
- ❖ Power Must Change Hands Vol.4: Arise and Shine
- ❖ Power Must Change Hands Vol.5: Family Restoration 1
- ❖ Power Must Change Hands Vol.6: Family Restoration 2
- ❖ Praying Like Jesus
- ❖ Conquering the Giant Called Poverty
- ❖ Generous Living
- ❖ Bind the Strongman
- ❖ Personal and Family Deliverance for You
- ❖ A Difference by Fire
- ❖ Your Time for Divine Expansion
- ❖ Jesus Our Jubilee
- ❖ The Choice of a Friend

- ❖ Christians and Politics
- ❖ Prayer Storm Daily Prayer Guide (monthly devotional)

For copies, contact your local books store or direct your request to:

Prayer Storm Team
P.O. Box 5018
Nkwen, Bamenda
Tel.: (237) 679465717 or 677436964
godsontnembo@gmail.com

Made in the USA
Columbia, SC
27 June 2025

59938224R00157